Maximizing the One-Shot

Maximizing the One-Shot

Connecting Library Instruction with the Curriculum

Jill Markgraf
Kate Hinnant
Eric Jennings
Hans Kishel

ROWMAN & LITTLEFIELD
Lanham • Boulder • New York • London

Published by Rowman & Littlefield
A wholly owned subsidiary of The Rowman & Littlefield Publishing Group, Inc.
4501 Forbes Boulevard, Suite 200, Lanham, Maryland 20706
www.rowman.com

Unit A, Whitacre Mews, 26-34 Stannary Street, London SE11 4AB

British Library Cataloguing in Publication Information Available

Library of Congress Cataloging-in-Publication Data

Markgraf, Jill, 1962–
  Maximizing the one-shot : connecting library instruction with the curriculum / Jill Markgraf, Kate Hinnant, Eric Jennings, Hans Kishel.
    pages cm
  Includes bibliographical references and index.
  ISBN 978-1-4422-3865-7 (cloth : alk. paper) – ISBN 978-1-4422-3866-4 (pbk. : alk. paper) – ISBN 978-1-4422-3867-1 (ebook) 1. Academic libraries–Relations with faculty and curriculum. 2. Information literacy–Study and teaching (Higher) 3. Library orientation for college students. 4. Research–Methodology–Study and teaching (Higher) I. Hinnant, Kate, 1970– II. Jennings, Eric, 1982– III. Kishel, Hans. IV. Title.
  Z675.U5M3373 2015
  025.5'677–dc23   2014048170

♾™ The paper used in this publication meets the minimum requirements of American National Standard for Information Sciences—Permanence of Paper for Printed Library Materials, ANSI/NISO Z39.48-1992.

Printed in the United States of America

Contents

Acknowledgments

When we were approached about turning our article on using Lesson Study in collaboration with English faculty published in *College & Research Libraries* into a book, we wondered whether or not we could do it. Each person on this team brought something to the table that made it possible, and we want to thank each other for all of the work that it took to put it together. When you have a great team, it makes tasks like this easier to accomplish.

We also want to thank our colleagues in McIntyre Library for encouraging us throughout this yearlong endeavor. We especially want to acknowledge our fellow instruction librarians, whose ongoing commitment to our one-shot curriculum has helped inspire this book. We thank our library director, John Pollitz, for his positivity and encouragement. Finally, a special note of gratitude goes to our colleagues at the University of Wisconsin–Eau Claire with whom we worked on the Lesson Study collaborations discussed in this book. We are fortunate to work with such committed faculty and are grateful for their thoughtful contributions to chapter 10 of this book: Bob Eierman, Shevaun Watson, Cathy Rex, Angie Stombaugh, Rita Sperstad, and Arin VanWormer.

Introduction

With a name that belongs in a John Wayne movie, and a reputation that elicits both resistance and celebration, the library one-shot instruction session is the subject of this book. Typically taught in a 50-minute period, the one-shot involves bringing a single class and a librarian together. Historically, the one-shot has run the gamut from covering library services to search tools to research strategies, using methods ranging from lectures and scavenger hunts to more open-ended active learning sessions.

In recent years, as librarians have devoted more attention to the assessment of their information literacy programs, the value of the one-shot library lesson has come into question. Article titles such as "Why One-Shot Information Literacy Sessions Are Not the Future of Instruction: A Case for Online Credit Courses" and "Life Beyond the One-Shot: Teaching a For-Credit Course" suggest a determination to move beyond the one-shot to information literacy programs that include credit courses, embedded librarianship, and other, more extended models.[1] At the same time, other researchers have focused on how assessment can be used to improve one-shot lessons[2] and how active learning can transform their nature.[3]

There are, of course, institutional factors that inform how likely it is that an academic library is going to transition from the one-shot to another form of library instruction: staffing, allocation of academic credits, instructional needs, and even space. And there can be no doubt that these factors are the primary reasons why the one-shot lesson is still a dominant form of library instruction.

But it is our contention that the one-shot is not a dead end. We argue instead that the one-shot can be cultivated into a dynamic lesson, responsive to the changes in the curriculum and scaffolded based on the needs and intellectual developments of the students. In this book, we describe the Lesson Study process that we used at the University of Wisconsin–Eau Claire, but we know that there are many approaches to lesson creation that promote the development of shared goals and objectives between librarians and disciplinary faculty. We argue that collaboration is an essential ingredient in making the one-shot a success. By taking a collaborative approach in the assessment and revision of their one-shots, librarians can raise their visibility as the go-to partners in inquiry instruction, whether at the first-year level or beyond.

DEFINITIONS

Throughout this book we use the term *information literacy* to refer to the broader goals and objectives involving finding, accessing, evaluating, creating, and responsibly using information. When we refer to the *library lesson*, we mean the individual one-shot lesson. Other information lessons, such as out-of-class assignments or information literacy lesson plans to be carried out by disciplinary faculty, are identified as such in the text. *Librarians* and *library faculty* are used interchangeably, though we realize that not every academic library uses faculty status for its librarians. *Team* refers to all members of a collaborative project or Lesson Study, including both librarians and disciplinary faculty.

THE BOOK

Though our book centers on our experience revising several one-shots, including lessons for first-year composition and nursing, we have tried to make what we have learned relevant to a wide variety of contexts. We describe our process, but also share guidelines and takeaways we have learned from both research and experience.

In chapter 1, we review the place of the one-shot within the history of information literacy in higher education. We also describe traditional one-shot formats, as well as the institutional constraints that make the one-shot prevalent as a mode of delivering library instruction. Finally, we outline the lack of curricular integration typical with one-shots.

Chapter 2 addresses the reasons for changing the way we approach the one-shot, as well as how to embark on such a project. Potential hurdles are discussed, and early decisions librarians need to make are laid out. Finally, there is a section on enacting transformational change.

Since collaboration is a large part of the process we describe, we devote the beginning of chapter 3 to identifying local institutional structures that can support a collaborative effort like one-shot revision. We also introduce Lesson Study, the process we used in revising several of our one-shots, and describe the planning phase of our first Lesson Study experience: a collaboration between the library and first-year composition instructors. In chapter 4, we continue the description of the Lesson Study method by describing how we taught and assessed our new first-year composition course's one-shot lesson, following up with revisions to the initial lesson.

Chapter 5 covers two additional Lesson Study projects our librarians completed with science faculty and nursing faculty, discussing the unique challenges of creating and revising disciplinarily based one-shots. We introduce the practice of scaffolding one-shots over multiple years for a single major, using the revision process to deliberately identify the developmental needs of students at every stage of their education.

In chapter 6, we discuss supplementing the one-shot with assignments and online lessons that disciplinary faculty can deploy in their classes. We also cover how to support faculty use of these materials in order to encourage their successful incorporation into the disciplinary faculty's curriculum.

Chapter 7 explores both the benefits and challenges of collaboration with faculty, focusing on recommended approaches to common scenarios. Organizational considerations are the subject of chapter 8, where we discuss networking, communicating with faculty, incentivizing collaboration, and assessing the one-shot.

In chapter 9 we address some of the particular challenges of the one-shot classroom experience. We begin with the tricky task of building rapport within minutes with each new class. Then we address leading meaningful discussion, which is often a common component of an active one-shot session. And in that chapter we address situations where the best-laid lesson plans often go awry and offer suggestions on how to recover when that happens.

Finally, because we view collaboration as so important to the successful design and implementation of a revised one-shot, we give over chapter 10 to six of the faculty we worked with during our Lesson Study process: two from English, three from nursing, and one from the Center for Excellence in Teaching and Learning. In their own words, they describe the benefits and challenges of collaborating on a one-shot revision project. They also describe the impact this collaboration has had on their pedagogy.

NOTES

1. Yvonne Mery, Jill Newby, and Ke Peng, "Why One-Shot Information Literacy Sessions Are Not the Future of Instruction: A Case for Online Credit Courses," *College & Research Libraries* 73, no. 4 (2012): 366–77, doi: 10.5860/crl-271; Amy Van Epps and Megan Sapp Nelson, "One-Shot or Embedded? Assessing Different Delivery Timing for Information Resources Relevant to Assignments," *Evidence Based Library & Information Practice* 8, no. 1 (2013): 4–18, http://ejournals.library.ualberta.ca/index.php/EBLIP/article/view/18027/14854; Mimi O'Maley, "Information Literacy Grown Up: One-Shot Instruction to Credit-Bearing Course," *Kentucky Libraries* 73, no. 4 (2009): 16–19; Lane Wilkinson and Virginia Cairns, "Life Beyond the One-Shot: Librarians Teaching a For-Credit Course," *Tennessee Libraries* 60, no. 3 (2010): 5.

2. Jacalyn E. Bryan and Elana Karshmer, "Assessment in the One-Shot Session: Using Pre- and Post-tests to Measure Innovative Instructional Strategies among First-Year Students," *College & Research Libraries* 74, no. 6 (2013): 574–86; Andrea Brooks, "Maximizing One-Shot Impact: Using Pre-Test Responses in the Information Literacy Classroom," *Southeastern Librarian* 61, no. 1 (2013): 41–43.

3. Van Houlson,"Getting Results from One-Shot Instruction: A Workshop for First-Year Students," *College & Undergraduate Libraries* 14, no. 1 (2007): 89–108. doi:10.1300/J106v14n01-07; Kevin Deemer, "Making the Most of the One-Shot You Got," *Community & Junior College Libraries* 14, no. 1 (2007): 21–26, doi:10.1300/J107v14n0104.

1

Confronting the One-Shot

Seeing the Limitations

WHY THE ONE-SHOT EXISTS

The one-shot library instruction session has often been regarded—and sometimes bemoaned—as the necessary compromise between a full-fledged information literacy course and nothing at all. It is viewed as the "one shot" librarians have with students. Librarians worry that the one-shot is not enough time to impart all the information students need to conduct meaningful research. Classroom faculty observe that students come to them with incomplete research skills, something they should have picked up somewhere, somehow along the way. Faculty are reluctant to give up more than a single class period—if even that—to something they feel students should be getting somewhere else. All of these factors lead librarians and faculty to a shared impression that the one-shot is not enough. And yet it persists as a prevalent model in many institutions of higher learning. Why?

The evolution of library instruction reflects trends not only in higher education but in society at large. Changes in higher education in the late 19th century prompted the growth of library instruction. The move from a classical and religious-based postsecondary education to a more secular and professional research-based emphasis in curricula led to changes that demanded an increased role in instruction for librarians: "the adoption of original research as a necessary function of academia, the introduction of the seminar method of instruction featuring student presentations, and the birth of new curricula in the social sciences and in professional and technical education."[1] Library instruction deemed necessary to support students in this new environment sometimes came in the form of a credit course, but evidence of what we now refer to as the one-shot also emerged. Otis Hall Robinson, a librarian at the University of Rochester, wrote in 1880 of his "lectures from time to time to freshman and sophomore classes" on using the library. Robinson noted the haphazard nature of these invitations to instruct: "These lectures or talks occur as opportunity offers, filling gaps when other professors are absent, or taking part of an hour now and then from his own regular class work."[2] Do these opportunities sound familiar?

Changes in higher education after World War II and into the 1960s led to a resurgence of interest in library education. The democratization of higher education put college into the reaches of populations heretofore excluded from the academy. Library systems designed to store materials and accommodate scholars had to serve a broader range of students who lacked skills in accessing and using bibliographic tools. Similarly, liberal education was evolving to emphasize inquiry and problem solving: "In the 1960s rigid curricula, lecture classes, and assigned research paper topics gave way to more independent study as faculties accommodated rebellious students."[3] A shift toward teaching what are now commonly referred to as critical-thinking skills was underway. A new wave of librarians, who had recently been those "rebellious students," was undaunted by shifting philosophies and curricula. They did what librarians always do and do best: they adapted. Once focused on the use of complex bibliographic tools and information-organization schemes and navigating physical collections, library instruction changed course when complex physical schema were replaced with complex online schema and protocols in the late 20th century. The tools have become more powerful and intuitive for the user in the early 21st century, forcing library instructors to adapt again and focus less on tools and more on the nature and use of the content itself. As students find it easier to access information, faculty, librarians, and even the students themselves seem to be in agreement that selection, evaluation, synthesis, integration, and ethical use of information are priorities in library instruction. And yet there is not a consensus within higher education on how and when these skills are best developed. Recognition of the need to develop broader skills in the use of information was reflected in a change in the terminology used to describe the type of instruction taking place in libraries. Bibliographic instruction, which emphasized the systematic skills of information retrieval, gradually gave way to "information literacy," a term that emerged in the 1970s and was codified by several organizations during the ensuing decades. In 1989, the American Library Association defined information literacy to guide the profession.[4] In 1998, "The Nine Information Literacy Standards for Student Learning" were released by the American Library Association and the Association for Educational Communications and Technology,[5] followed in 2000 by the Association of College & Research Libraries (ACRL) development of the "Information Literacy Competency Standards for Higher Education."[6]

Much effort has focused on increasing information literacy instruction in higher education, and the models vary widely, with new approaches constantly evolving, each with its own set of strengths and weaknesses. Library instruction programs have manifested themselves in a number of ways over the years:

- *One-shot*: This is typically a 50-minute visit of a librarian to a classroom, or of a class to a library teaching space, in which a librarian demonstrates how to use the library. These sessions have evolved over time and have focused on everything from teaching the use of print bibliographic tools, the physical layout of libraries, and the navigation of complex protocol-dependent online technologies to focusing on the content rather than the finding tools. These sessions may "occur as opportunity offers," as simply a means to filling a class period or providing a general tour or overview of using the library. Ideally, they are integrated into the course, offered at the point of need rather than as an introduction at the beginning of a semester.

- *Stand-alone courses*: These courses might be credit-bearing or not, in person or online. They may be required courses, or they may be electives. These courses require planning, commitment, and support not only by the library but by the entire institution. The demands posed by this approach keep it from being as widespread as the ubiquitous one-shot.
- *Workshops or drop-in sessions*: These are ad hoc offerings, perhaps one-off classes or a series of sessions, that librarians offer to whomever wishes to attend. They are not connected to a particular course but are sometimes geared toward specific groups, such as graduate students, students in a particular discipline, international students, or nontraditional students.
- *Handouts*: Usually created for a specific task or concept, the ever-popular handout has taken many forms. One example was the pathfinder, which led students through processes and highlighted sources for researching specific topics. Handouts are less popular now than in the past, as much of the content has gone online or taken other forms.
- *Self-guided workbooks*: These allow students to work at their own pace. Self-guided instruction can be assigned by instructors, required for graduation, or be optional. This model is easily scalable, with the potential to be used by any number of students. However, the generic nature that makes this format scalable also poses a drawback in that it can feel disconnected from specific information needs and runs the risk of being viewed as busywork.
- *Online "full-length" tutorials*: This model was extremely popular in the 1990s and largely usurped the role of workbooks. The technology offered greater interactivity and multimedia options. The best-known example is the Texas Information Literacy Tutorial (TILT),[7] a modular, web-based library research tool that incorporates humor, interactivity, some degree of personalization, and assessment of comprehension. Developed at the University of Texas, it was shared with and adapted by libraries throughout the world. While this and similar models are still in use, enthusiasm for these long, all-inclusive tutorials waned in the mid-2000s and gave way to shorter point-of-need tutorials or learning objects.
- *Embeddable learning objects*: These tools are designed to demonstrate a specific process or concept. They may come in the form of text, short video content, or other multimedia content. Screen capture software such as Jing or Camtasia makes the development of these objects quick and easy for librarians. They can

be carefully crafted objects or created on the fly as needed, and they are easily embedded into web pages or courseware by instructors.

- *Interactive tutorials*: Online tutorial applications such as Guide on the Side, developed at the University of Arizona,[8] combine real search capability, rather than simulation, with accompanying instructions. They provide an online tutorial experience that is more personalized and customizable to a student's interest and attempt to better reflect an authentic search experience.
- *Embedded librarians in online courses*: As instruction moved online, so did the way librarians communicate and work with students. The extent to which librarians are embedded in courses varies widely, with librarians working as co-instructors in a course or perhaps fielding occasional research-related questions in a discussion thread. How integral the librarian can be in a course—or several courses—is a factor of many conditions, not the least of which is the level of librarian staffing and the expectations for librarian involvement.
- *Train-the-trainer*: Another method of offering information literacy instruction that addresses the problem of limited librarian staffing is that in which librarians train others, often the instructors themselves, to include information literacy concepts into their teaching.
- *One-on-one consultations*: The personal approach to information literacy instruction, a mainstay in librarianship, cannot be overlooked. Each interaction at the reference desk or appointment in a librarian's office is a form of instruction, arguably the most effective but also the least scalable to an entire student body.

This list is not exhaustive, as librarians continue to come up with unique and innovative ways to work with students. On some campuses, a library instruction component is required for graduation; on others it is an elective. Some library instruction models incorporate graduate students or support staff in teaching; others restrict teaching to librarians. Some models are heavily lecture- or text-based, while others are interactive. Some models emphasize the procedural steps in acquiring information, and others encourage exploration and inquiry. Models used at various institutions are driven by such factors as campus and library history and culture; budgets and staffing levels; experience, innovation, and teaching philosophies of the librarians and faculty; and relationships between librarians and others on campus.

Many librarians and instructors lament that most of these models are insufficient to convey the depth and breadth of information literacy concepts to students. As a result, some regard the full-blown credit-bearing course as the holy grail of information literacy instruction. However, it has its supporters and detractors. Thomas Eland, a proponent of the information literacy course, argues that "to be effective, information literacy instruction must be integrated into our institutions in the same way that all instruction is integrated."[9] Librarians, he states, are the information literacy experts and, as thus, should be afforded a status that enables them to have control over the curriculum, to study it, teach it, and assess its outcomes. However, adding information literacy courses to a college curriculum can be an onerous endeavor, requiring buy-in from the entire campus, an economic model that can sustain the addition of such a course, and librarians' time and expertise to develop and offer the course. Such courses have mixed results. While the ability to delve into information literacy concepts more deeply can have positive outcomes, the credit-course model is not without its problems. Such courses can feel disconnected from authentic information needs. Students may regard them as unnecessary expenditures of their time and tuition dollars. Other students see them as "easy" courses with which to fill a schedule.

Barbara Fister is less enthusiastic about an information literacy stand-alone course and outlines a compelling defense of the one-shot approach, which she refers to as course-related library instruction. Recognizing the limitations of a "single fifty-minute window of opportunity to reach students . . . dependent on individual faculty inviting librarians to be involved," she states that the one-shot nevertheless "embraces a fundamental assumption of course-related instruction; that faculty in the disciplines are key players in information literacy instruction. . . . In fact, it assumes the single 'shot' a librarian has with the students is accompanied by a far more thorough exposure to research skills provided by the instructor throughout the course."[10] In this statement, Fister challenges a negative yet pervasive interpretation of the one-shot. A librarian may meet with a class on just one occasion, but that does not mean that all information literacy efforts begin and end with that one visit.

There is no shortage of information literacy models from which to choose, and no dearth of opinions on the efficacy of each. What is irrefutable, however, is that the one-shot model persists in part because of the sheer pragmatism of the model. Many academic institutions are set up to support this model, and academic institutions do not change quickly or easily. They represent, if not the ideal, the reality of many institutions. According to the National Center for Education Statistics, in 2012, the average number of librarians and professional staff per 1,000 full-time equivalent (FTE) was 3.97. In 2012, the median number of librarians and professional staff per 1,000 students was 2.27.[11] Considering these ratios, it is not feasible for librarians at many institutions to have more face time with students.

WHAT THE ONE-SHOT HAS TYPICALLY DONE

Even within the one-shot there are many variations on what can be taught and how it should be taught. Typical one-shot instruction sessions fall into the following categories:

- How to use specific tools (e.g., a database, catalog, citation software)
- How to do specific tasks (e.g., cite sources properly, borrow items from other libraries, write a literature review)
- Research concepts (e.g., generating keywords, evaluating sources for their usefulness, synthesizing information)

- Library orientation tours (e.g., what are the different parts of the library, how to check out materials, how to get help in the library)

One-shot instruction can also be taught in a variety of ways. A traditionally popular model is a lecture in which a librarian demonstrates search processes and students may or may not follow along on screen or on a computer. Adopting pedagogical innovation, some librarians use a flipped classroom, in which the students obtain content knowledge outside of class. The flipped library session can then be devoted to student exploration and discussion. A hybrid session combines lecture and active learning in a session, comprising minimal instruction followed by independent student work assisted by a librarian.

Where instruction takes place is also variable. Some colleges and universities have dedicated lab space they use for library instruction. Others use mobile devices like laptops and iPads to transform an area of the library into a de facto lab. A third possibility is for librarians to meet with a class in its regular classroom. That room may be a lab, or students may bring their own devices. Though it is increasingly the norm for library instruction to include the use of a computer for students, not every session does.

The typical one-shot library instruction session takes place in the library and tries to pack multiple aspects of information literacy into one 50-minute session.[12] Before this session, librarians promise the moon and stars to faculty members, even while recognizing that what is asked cannot actually be accomplished in a short period of time. Because librarians try to accomplish so much in a short amount of time, there is little time for active learning, and, as a result, most of the class session is lecture-based. And with so much content to process, students have difficulty distinguishing between what is crucial and what is secondary.

According to Bligh in his writing on the efficacy of various teaching methods: "Lectures are as effective as other methods to teach facts."[13] Yet, within the 21st-century college classroom setting, educators are encouraged to move away from lectures and to active learning. Why? It is true that some of what might occur within a traditional library one-shot session involves teaching facts and thus can be facilitated through a lecture. However, one cannot read about or be taught the concept of information literacy for 50 minutes and subsequently become information literate. For students to become information literate, they need time and practice, neither of which are afforded in a 50-minute session. In that time frame, it is impossible for librarians to teach essential connections between research and writing.[14]

One-shot sessions are often scripted: librarians use canned searches to describe how to find a book, article, or other item. These searches make the process seem quite simple and linear. Words are input, results are returned, and inevitably one of the items on that results list is exactly what the theoretical searcher is looking for. In reality, as students soon experience, searching is recursive and may require multiple methods of retrieving information: the library catalog, article databases, different keywords or phrases, use of subject headings or limiters, and so on. They are given a false sense of order and effortlessness that falls apart the minute they leave class and try to research on their own. The process is messy and hard to represent in a lecture format. Librarians and faculty aren't able to give students the time to explore the messiness of searching. And when students encounter issues in their searching, they are tempted to short-circuit the process by bailing out of their topic or settling with the results they get.

In addition to being scripted, the one-shot sometimes focuses on specific tools such as the library catalog or an article database. Specific tools are taught because librarians are working toward the goal of getting students to the right materials for their assignment. In certain instances, there may be only one search tool that gets students what they need, and they have to master it for the purposes of their assignment. However, by presenting only that preselected tool, librarians skip over teaching the essential step of tool discovery and selection. The tool-based one-shot methodology is also problematic because library search tools are not static; they come and go and change regularly. When students are focused on the tool rather than on search concepts, they are unable to adapt or transfer skills to other search situations.

Unfortunately not all one-shot instruction sessions are tied to particular assignments requiring information literacy skills. Faculty members schedule library sessions without such assignments for several reasons. In some cases, faculty are gone for a conference and know that librarians will accept the opportunity to teach a library instruction session. It becomes, by default, a substitute teaching service so that faculty can have coverage when they are gone. In other instances, faculties use library instruction to fill a gap in the syllabus even if the timing of the session is not coordinated with student need. In these scenarios, students tend not to be engaged. Unless students are aware of the instrumental reasons for learning research concepts or skills, it is hard for them to see the relevance of library sessions divorced from assignments.

Given the variations in circumstances surrounding library instruction, librarians have had to adapt. For example, librarians are often asked to cover multiple information literacy objectives in a single lesson. When asked, librarians often will acquiesce to the faculty member, trying to cover all that is asked even when not reasonable for a 50-minute one-shot session. A contrasting scenario, in which the librarian determines what will take place in the one-shot session, may result in a prepackaged lesson. This might save a librarian time in preparation, but it doesn't allow for the important give-and-take between a librarian and faculty member. In both of these instances, the lack of a conversation between librarian and faculty member can make the library instruction session less effective because a shared understanding of the class session's objectives is never forged.

As was briefly mentioned above, the timing of the library instruction session is an important factor in its success. Too early in the semester and students will still be trying to figure out the expectations of the course and the professor, and won't be concerned about library research. Additionally, if it is too early, they may not remember what they learned when it needs to be applied for class assignments. Too late in the semester and students will be focused on finishing the class successfully, forced into a just-in-time research situation, and unable to see the connection between what they're learning and the overall objectives of the class.

INSTITUTIONAL REALITIES SET LIMITS

It is hard not to approach the one-shot from within a framework informed by tradition, restricted by institutional realities and overburdened with internal and external expectations. Making significant changes to the one-shot or pushing against the limitations in the one-shot paradigm can seem radical, which is a testament to the forces that shape the one-shot's staying power as a flawed yet constant fixture in higher education.

In many cases, the institutional factors described earlier in this chapter shape the way librarians view the one-shot. Because many colleges and universities are operating without a programmatic approach to information literacy that is supported across the institution, the one-shot is often used to fill a gap in the curriculum. As a result, librarians often view the one-shot as their only chance to reach students. They must bank everything on this one exchange, because, without institutional planning for the inclusion of information literacy throughout the curriculum, they may never see them again. Depending on their major, students' exposure to library-based inquiry may be extensive or nonexistent.

The reality of the one-shot as a stand-alone session, not as an intentionally planned and integrated class, puts library instructors in the position of drawing up goals and objectives for students in a near vacuum. Because many faculty members consider information literacy instruction to be the domain of librarians, collaboration for one-shots is not common. Instead, faculty "give up" a class session for the library instruction. It is then the librarians' responsibility to figure out how to maximize the hour or so they have to accomplish the information literacy inoculation the students need. Course syllabi, familiarity with the major, and past experiences all help, but it is rare to find faculty who have the time to discuss their class. And in a setting where information literacy instruction is achieved on an ad hoc basis, there is no way to determine when or if students will ever receive library instruction again during the course of their college career. Students also come with a variety of information literacy backgrounds. It is difficult to assess, for the purposes of a one-shot, what they already know.

Often library instruction is offered in the first year of college, when it is considered vital in bridging students' high school experience with the more demanding expectations of college work. But many faculty members also request library instruction when majors are working on capstones or large research projects.

Some limits are imposed by circumstances and institutional constraints, but other limitations come from collectively imposed expectations. Librarians saddle themselves with the idea that students should come out of one session being somewhere close to "information literate." While librarians rationally understand that becoming information literate is a lifetime process, they still find themselves examining the wide range of objectives represented in the ACRL competencies, wondering how many they can help students achieve in one 50-minute session. Academic librarians are in the structurally challenging position of being both academic and service staff. They must juggle the competing obligations of professional academic standards with the imperative to provide service in a manner that ensures repeat customers.

Another limitation that commonly prevents departments or units from tackling programmatic change to classes or lessons is the tension between protecting the academic freedom to choose teaching goals, methods, and styles and the imperative to meet collectively determined goals and objectives. Working together to make sure that the aims of the one-shot lesson are clear and justified, as well as widely shared, can help overcome resistance to adopting a library-wide approach.

In addition to institutional and professional considerations, the very nature of the one-shot classroom experience can limit the sense of what is possible for librarians. Perhaps most importantly, with one 50-minute session it is very difficult to develop relationships with students. This can inhibit discussion in class, as well as limit the librarian's ability to assess the needs of the class or of individual students. Thus, the practice of teaching to the lowest common denominator becomes a given in many one-shot situations. And while some faculty members are careful to brief library instructors on the assignment and what the students have done to prepare for it, very often librarians have to walk into one-shot sessions blind, not knowing at what stage the students are in their process.

THE LACK OF INTEGRATION: THE GOAL OF RELEVANCE

One of the larger challenges in teaching one-shot library sessions is conveying the relevance of the content to the students' work in the course and in their undergraduate careers. While this can often be stymied by ill-timed one-shot sessions, coming at a time when students are not prepared or expected to begin their research, it is also a challenge even when course instructors have taken pains to prepare their students with assignments and preparatory work. Without contextualizing the one-shot and knitting it closely with the assignment or skill the students are pursuing, it is easy for the one-shot to seem like a blip on the horizon of their semester. Too often students see what they learned in a library session as being external to the curriculum, that is, content to be consulted when the research paper comes around, but not related to the course content. And though research has shown that many disciplinary faculty members theoretically prioritize information literacy instruction, they don't necessarily incorporate it into their own teaching.[15]

The integration of information literacy into academic curricula has long been a goal of academic librarians. In the "Information Literacy and Pedagogy" section of ACRL's *Information Literacy Competency Standards for Higher Education*, the potential scope of integration is laid out: "Achieving competency in information literacy requires an understanding that this cluster of abilities is not extraneous to the curriculum but is woven into the curriculum's content, structure, and sequence."[16] Thus, rather than presenting instruction isolated from content or by a temporary and nontransferable need, information literacy is planned into the course and made evident not just by librarians but by faculty and course content as well. Several librarians have connected integration specifically with embedded librarianship,[17] but that is not the only instructional framework. With planning, one-shot instruction can be woven into a course in a way that intentionally marries content, purpose, and skills.

Integrating information literacy instruction requires collaboration with faculty so that the one-shot is orchestrated to fit timewise and goalwise into the course. But even more ideal, this collaboration should result in the course adoption of information literacy objectives in a meaningful and progressive way. Our work at the University of Wisconsin–Eau Claire in rethinking the one-shot began with this kind of effort, integrating information literacy into the new campus composition program. But integration can go beyond a single course. In nursing, we have designed scaffolded instruction so that the one-shots the students take become more advanced as they progress through their major. Because this string of one-shots is designed to go along with the specific assignments students are engaged in, the relevance of each one-shot is clear to the students.

In order to achieve truly programmatic changes to library instruction, it helps to have buy-in. Integration requires collaboration between more than one librarian and faculty member; multiple collaborators help consider the full course, major, or program so that the one-shot is incorporated into the curriculum intentionally and authentically. In order to promote programmatic consistency, collaboration is key to developing shared philosophies among teaching librarians.

Such collaboration requires dialogue about learning goals, and not just those clearly defined as information literacy objectives. By being frank about expectations, participants can begin to prioritize what can actually be accomplished in a one-shot versus what is desired. We, like many library instructors, wanted to get away from the super-crammed lecture format and move toward a model of the one-shot as an active learning experience. It was only by thinking through our objectives and the many ways we could get our students to achieve them that we became open to real one-shot change.

NOTES

1. Otis Hall Robinson, "College Libraries as Aids to Instruction: Rochester University Library-Administration and Use," in *User Instruction in Academic Libraries: A Century of Selected Readings*, ed. Larry L. Hardesty, John P. Schmitt, and John Mark Tucker (Metuchen, NJ: Scarecrow Press, 1986), 3.

2. Ibid., 26.

3. Donald J. Kenney, "Assessing Library Instruction: Where It Has Been and Where Is It Taking Us?" *Catholic Library World* 59, no. 1 (1987): 41.

4. American Library Association, "Presidential Committee on Information Literacy: Final Report" (white paper, 1989), http://www.ala.org/acrl/publications/whitepapers/presidential.

5. American Association of School Librarians and Association for Educational Communications and Technology, *Information Power: Building Partnerships for Learning* (Chicago: American Library Association, 1998), 8–9.

6. Association of College & Research Libraries, *Information Literacy Competency Standards for Higher Education* (Chicago: Association of College & Research Libraries, 2000), http://www.ala.org/acrl/files/standards/standards.pdf.

7. "Texas Information Literacy Tutorial," University of Texas Libraries, http://tilt.lib.utsystem.edu/ (site discontinued).

8. "Guide on the Side," University of Arizona Libraries, accessed December 12, 2013, http://code.library.arizona.edu/gots.

9. Barbara Fister and Thomas Eland, "Curriculum Issues in Information Literacy Instruction," in *Information Literacy Instruction Handbook*, ed. Christopher N. Cox and Elizabeth Blakesley Lindsay (Chicago: Association of College & Research Libraries, 2008), 106.

10. Ibid., 94–95.

11. "Compare Academic Libraries," National Center for Educational Statistics, accessed December 16, 2013, http://nces.ed.gov/surveys/libraries/compare/.

12. The authors recognize that one-shot library sessions vary in length depending on institution and class scheduling. Because 50 minutes is the norm at the authors' institution, it will be used to represent the typical session in this book.

13. Donald A. Bligh, *What's the Use of Lectures?* (San Francisco: Jossey-Bass Publishers, 2000), 4.

14. Heidi L. M. Jacobs and Dale Jacobs, "Transforming the One-Shot Library Session into Pedagogical Collaboration: Information Literacy and the English Composition Class," *Reference & User Services Quarterly* 49, no. 1 (2009): 11, doi:10.5860/rusq.49n1.72.

15. Sophie Bury, "Faculty Attitudes, Perceptions and Experiences of Information Literacy: A Study across Multiple Disciplines at York University, Canada," *Journal of Information Literacy* 5, no. 1 (2011): 53–54, doi: 10.11645/5.1.1513.

16. Association of College & Research Libraries, 5.

17. Norma G. Kobzina, "A Faculty–Librarian Partnership: A Unique Opportunity for Course Integration," *Journal of Library Administration* 50, no. 4 (2010): 294–95, doi: 10.1080/01930821003666965; Li Wang, "An Information Literacy Integration Model and Its Application in Higher Education," *Reference Services Review* 39, no. 4 (2011): 704.

2

Getting Real About the One-Shot

Once you've decided that you want different results from your one-shot, it is time to get real about making that change in a deliberate and thorough way. There is an increasing body of library literature that addresses rethinking the one-shot and makes recommendations for achieving change.

But why the emphasis on changing the one-shot? And why now? One reason for this focus stems from the broader changes in academia in recent years and decades. Many campuses and libraries have seen dramatic changes in their infrastructures, offering teaching and learning opportunities that didn't exist before. Not all that long ago it was uncommon for librarians to have access to a teaching lab. Teaching spaces that accommodated the lecture model were commonplace. With the addition of teaching labs, including a workstation for every student, came the ability for students to engage with content in a way they were previously unable to. The maturation of databases, catalogs, resource discovery layers, and other search tools available in libraries meant more intuitive interfaces, requiring less teaching time devoted to navigating the cumbersome protocols of individual tools.

Beyond the physical and technological changes taking place in libraries, other transformations were taking place on college campuses. The scholarship of teaching and learning was becoming more valued, creating a greater interest among faculty in exploring teaching and learning methods. This development has resulted in more research on and attention paid to teaching and learning styles. At the same time, college campuses are seeing shifting demographics that are becoming more inclusive, with students more diverse in age, ethnicity, range of abilities, economic background, and academic preparedness than ever before. Within this diversified population, some learners present new needs that have to be met by introducing more inclusive teaching approaches.

To be clear, within this context, it is not as if librarians have been standing still. Library lessons are continuously tweaked and revised. But a more radical revision, rethinking the priorities and methods of the one-shot, is what we are addressing in this book. It is always risky to introduce change. In the case of the one-shot, if the lesson fails, the faculty member may not invite the librarian back. He or she may decide that including time for library instruction in the syllabus just isn't worth it. However, librarians are also aware that to resist change is not an option. To resist change is to become irrelevant and ultimately obsolete. And so, even though it can be risky, librarians must be constantly reevaluating and recalibrating what they do and how they do it. Teaching the one-shot is no exception. While librarians do risk alienating some faculty members by introducing content or a pedagogical style that deviates from past practice, it is equally possible that they lose the support of faculty members who see our current content as growing stale and out of touch. If faculty observe librarians providing routine and static instruction semester after semester, they may feel they know it so well that they can deliver that content without involving the librarian.

While a train-the-trainer model is not inherently undesirable in all situations, for librarians to relinquish the role of primary information literacy instruction is not in the best interest of the students. Librarians are the experts when it comes to selecting, accessing, and navigating the ever-changing array of information sources available. Faculty members are unequivocally the content experts in their disciplines. They have developed research strategies that have enabled them to be successful and have honed these strategies as they developed expertise in their field. They are intimately familiar with the terminology, journals, and authorities in their field, and this knowledge enables them to use search strategies that are different from those who are new to the field. According to William Badke, many faculty members are so immersed in their fields' literature that they may not even need to use the search tools that are integral for undergraduate research.[1] Because they have developed strategies that work for them, faculty are not necessarily focused on following and adapting to changes in the way information is accessed and managed, as are librarians. Nor are they necessarily familiar with information sources outside of their disciplines that may be of use to their students. So, instruction librarians cannot afford to let a perception take hold that they are superfluous. To do so poses a greater risk—ultimately to the students we serve—than introducing change.

GETTING STARTED

One of the first steps in this process is getting over the almost immobilizing mental hurdle the one-shot presents. Library literature is rife with critiques of the one-shot session.[2] The limitations described by librarians and outlined in chapter 1 make it easy to undervalue the one-shot instruction session. However, in order to surmount this mental hurdle, we must reframe perceived limitations as opportunities. In fact, many of the perceptions that constrain librarians in their thinking about the one-shot instruction session, such as the fact that we are guests in someone else's class or that there isn't enough time to teach everything that we want to teach, can be positives.

Librarians often perceive that students see them as strangers in a negative way: interlopers in the students' familiar class.[3] In some instances, this may be true. However, it also can be positive. For one, librarians don't grade students in the one-shot session. By removing the pressure of performing for a grade, students can focus on learning the concepts being taught in the one-shot session. Additionally, because librarians only see students once, having someone come to the classroom breaks up the monotony of having the same person teach a class day after day. Students may be excited by the prospect of a guest speaker. If the reason that the librarian is there is directly tied to an assignment and it is clear to the students from the outset that they will benefit, teaching the one-shot can be productive for the librarian and student. Finally, going to the library or having a librarian come to a class for an instruction session can reduce library anxiety in students.[4] This barrier, whether it is manifested in a physical or mental anxiety, is real. Helping reduce it is, in and of itself, reason enough to continue teaching the one-shot instruction session.

There is no denying that the time constraints of the one-shot, which are frequently disparaged, constitute a challenge. But having more time does not necessarily mean that the library instruction will be better. Pushing for a semester-long information literacy course taught by a librarian, for example, isn't always an institutional possibility. Even without considering financial and personnel concerns, it should be noted that faculty are often comfortable with the existing schema, and if librarians were to discontinue the one-shot in favor of a stand-alone course, it may actually do more harm than good. How? If the one-shot library instruction session is done properly, it can tie directly into course goals or an assignment that makes the instruction more effective. Without that direct tie-in, students may have to rely on library skills learned a semester or years before and independently draw connections between that course and others.

One benefit of constructing a one-shot session within a time constraint is that it can compel librarians and faculty to distill the content down to the most salient points. Focusing the content will make the instruction session better: the one-shot is no longer a laundry list of things that need to be covered. Rather, the librarian can use multiple methods of instruction to cover one or two key concepts. Assuming that students will be exposed to one-shot sessions in multiple courses, this approach acknowledges the way students learn: not everything all at once, but by building skills and concepts over time.

By using the time constraint of the one-shot to frame the conversation, the librarian can confer with faculty over priorities for the lesson in terms of effective use of the class time. This brings the purpose of the instruction session to the fore. Although one study indicated that only 11 percent of faculty collaborated with a librarian in design and evaluation of library assignments,[5] it does not mean that 89 percent are not collaborating in other ways. In many cases they are likely discussing the library lesson itself. For example, the librarian may suggest to the faculty member a new approach, such as introducing keyword concepts prior to having the students jump right into searching. Or a faculty member may ask the librarian to place more emphasis on citation chasing (i.e., using bibliographies to find further research) rather than just focusing on library databases. Recognizing together that everything cannot be covered in a 50-minute class period and then prioritizing content for students illustrates how time constraints can evoke conversations that make the one-shot a collaborative experience. If the time constraint is explicitly addressed in this conversation, librarians and faculty will better understand what each can reasonably expect from a one-shot. In other words, the librarian and faculty member can come to a mutual understanding that students will not emerge from a one-shot as information literate, but that becoming information literate is a learning process that requires time and recursive effort.

The conversation that takes place between librarians and faculty enables them both to approach the instruction session with shared expectations. Faculty are in a position to better prepare their students for the library instruction session. If they know what is to be covered during the session, they can make sure that their students are at a point where the content will be relevant. The students will be more engaged if they understand how the library session supports the work they are doing in class, and the librarian will have an easier time making sure that the concepts that are the focus of the class resonate. For the librarian, understanding what is expected in the class and for a given assignment, as well as having some familiarity with the terminology and concepts emphasized in the class, makes it easier to tailor remarks and examples to the specific needs of the students.

Finally, the term "one-shot" suggests that this one instruction session is the librarian's *only* shot to teach information literacy skills to students. While it may not be possible to remove "one-shot" from librarians' lexicon, we need to remember that the one-shot really isn't the only time librarians work with students. Librarians can introduce information literacy concepts to students in many places: in any subsequent library instruction session a student may attend; at the reference desk; in their offices; via chat, text, IM, and telephone; as roving librarians in the library or on campus; embedded in course management systems, via videoconferencing techniques like Skype, and many more. Acknowledging that all of these different options exist for student-librarian interaction should enable a librarian to regard the one-shot in a more positive light.

EARLY QUESTIONS

Deciding to take on the challenge of revamping the one-shot requires developing specific goals and objectives. But before that happens, there are broader pedagogical considerations to address about the optimal learning environment, student engagement, and the roles of students, librarians, and faculty in the learning experience. The answers to these questions fall short of being actual concrete lesson goals and objectives. However, they are an important step along the way in envisioning the revised session and formalizing goals and objectives.

Since the 1980s, educators have experimented with ways to support the diverse learning styles students bring to the classroom. This has been the impetus for pedagogical change at levels from kindergarten through college. In a 2004 study, authors Coffield et al. identified 71 models of learning styles.[6] In one popular construct that distilled learning styles to their most basic elements, learners were described as auditory, those who learn best by hearing; kinesthetic, those who learn best by doing; or visual, those who learn best by seeing. It would be impractical if not impossible for librarians to become intimately familiar with all current learning style models, just as it would be impossible to assess the learning styles of each student with whom they interact. The librarian's best strategy is to include several teaching modes likely to hit a broad swath of learning styles. To this end, active learning practices can help guide librarians in their quest to vary their pedagogical plans.

For many librarians, a change in teaching style is likely to involve a shift from a lecture-heavy, instructor-centric model to a more active learning, student-centered model. Though active learning has surged in importance at all levels of education, it is nothing new; in fact it can found in the teaching of the Greeks and the Socratic method[7]: through questioning, students were encouraged to develop their own informed responses to the moral and epistemological issues Socrates proposed. Elizabeth Barkley, who describes active learning as happening when "students make information or a concept their own by connecting it to their existing knowledge and experience," offers a more contemporary definition.[8]

Many see active learning's recent upsurge as a direct response to the historical institutionalization of education, particularly since the rise of the medieval university, in which learning became more formalized, moving away from the back and forth of the Socratic method and toward a model of the student as the empty and passive vessel, waiting to be filled with knowledge by expert tutors and lecturers. Paulo Freire's essay "The Banking Concept of Education" is well known for damning this form of education as the enemy of creative, critical thinking.[9]

Though active learning practices have been employed for years, it was not until the Study Group on the Conditions of Excellence in American Higher Education, under the aegis of the U.S. Department of Education, published a national report in 1984 giving recommendations for the improvement of higher education and calling for the use of active-learning methods, that the higher education community took an active interest in this pedagogical shift.[10] And though there is no centrally agreed-upon definition of active learning, proponents advocate for creating an environment for students in higher education to take a more active role in their own education, shifting away from primarily lower-order activities, such as memorization, to higher-order thinking. A key component of active learning is student engagement, which is achieved through a number of means, including reading, reflection, and the use of learning activities in addition to or at the exclusion of class lectures.[11]

Because the one-shot usually precedes a project in which students are about to conduct their own research, making active choices in selection, analysis, and synthesis of their sources, pedagogy that promotes active learning is an ideal match. Lessons that allow students to construct knowledge from experience and reflection can be directly useful to the student's coursework.

But active learning is not synonymous with activity in learning. It is not a given that a classroom discussion or group project will, by default, engage all students. Likewise, for some students a lecture can create an authentic active learning experience: "highly skilled listeners who are involved in a lecture by self-questioning, analyzing, and incorporating new information into their existing knowledge are learning more actively than students who are participating in a small group discussion that is off-task, redundant, or superfluous."[12]

Library instruction literature is replete with strategies for incorporating activity into teaching. What are less developed are strategies for eliciting authentic learning from the activities. Offering various modes of teaching in a 50-minute session can be challenging for the librarian. But doing so increases the opportunities for a greater number of students to engage with concepts.

Another consideration for the revised lesson is how research itself will be presented. All library instruction has an approach to research, though sometimes these approaches are unarticulated and inherent, rather than explicit parts of the lessons. As mentioned earlier, a common approach to the one-shot, in which searching the catalog and databases is demonstrated to students, can often impart the sense that research is a discrete set of retrieval tasks, conducted in a stepwise fashion. This serves to separate the content of research from the actual task of finding that content, reducing research to a process similar to looking up movies on Netflix, only with a more powerful search interface.

To ameliorate the disconnect between the "task" of searching and research itself, many librarians also introduce the concept of research as a process (see figure 2.1). In the 1970s and '80s, composition instructors began teaching "writing as a process." Introducing research as a process dovetailed nicely with this pedagogical paradigm.

However, talking about researching as a process is one thing; having students understand what that means in 50 minutes is another, particularly if librarians are focusing most of the period on the search "task" instructions. In trying to pair these

Figure 2.1.   Research and writing are commonly taught as processes.

two approaches to research, the "research as a process" message often has been undermined by the focus on individual steps.

Another issue with research as a process is how the librarian represents that process. When simplified for the purposes of a diagram, the steps in the process can seem like another set of tasks for the students, not unlike a step-by-step list of instructions. The challenge is in representing the process as the messy one that it is, without losing the effectiveness of the model as a teaching tool. Understanding the recursive and nonlinear nature of research is more effective when experienced rather than described, which is why having students do actual research during the one-shot is a potent option.

Spending some time thinking about the perceptions students will have about research, what it entails, and how best it is done, is an important step in visualizing the change you want in your one-shot. But skills are still important to the one-shot. Skills are often the main focus of course design and revision. Librarians often have an idea, supplemented by faculty, of things they want students to be able to do: request a book by ILL, cite a source, find a newspaper article. Sometimes drawing up skills constitutes the main part of course design. In redesigning the one-shot, it is important not to get caught up in skills-dominant pedagogy, but instead to think about how the desired skills fit into information literacy. One way to refocus the discussion of what skills students should learn in a one-shot is to consider how skills can be taught to enhance their transferability. Other approaches include farming some skills back out to the regular classroom or to out-of-class learning objects, or reconsidering skills in a progression that may begin but not end with the one-shot.

How to engage students is another worthy consideration. This may involve active-learning practices, but it is certainly not limited to them. As librarians know, students get more out of library sessions when they have something at stake. Having an assignment, doing some preparatory work on topics and research questions, and knowing faculty expectations can all help students find library lessons more meaningful. In one-shot revision, figuring out how to make such arrangements compulsory rather than up to chance can be a significant programmatic shift.

If major changes are made to the one-shot—to its structure, style, and content—then it stands to reason that the role of the librarian also changes. How that role is envisioned may determine the type of activity that occurs during the session. Is the librarian there to dispense information, to coach, to guide? If an active learning approach is desired, what is the role of the librarian in interacting with the students and the knowledge they create? Is the librarian a moderator, synthesizer, or even rectifier? The changing role that the librarian takes can also lead to a different relationship between the librarian and the students. If librarians leave center stage and conduct one-shots primarily among students, they may appear less like representatives of the library and more like partners to the students.

Related to the role of the librarian is how the students will connect with the library once the one-shot is over. Seeing a librarian in their midst, assisting students, encouraging their ideas and choices, helps demonstrate that librarians are not just dispensers of information but also willing collaborators in student work. Librarians can underline this role by emphasizing their availability for consultations outside of class and making clear the types of assistance they can provide.

Improving the one-shot can have benefits not just for students but for the librarians who teach the classes also. As we will discuss in the next few chapters, collaborating with faculty on the lesson redesign is a good way to band together to address goals and frustrations in a way that forges stronger relationships with faculty. But even if a cross-disciplinary team is not a possibility, regular communication with faculty about the one-shot lesson can strengthen the librarians' relationship with faculty. In sharing the intentional, thought-out rationale for changes in one-shot instruction, librarians have the chance to demonstrate how the revised lesson can better serve both students and faculty.

The revision process is also the time to clearly communicate what expectations are realistic for the one-shot. While the main audience for this is faculty who request the one-shot, formally asserting these expectations is also valuable for the teaching librarians themselves. Instead of laboring under the unrealistic obligation to try to research-proof students in one session, librarians can feel confident that their revised lesson contains realistic and achievable goals.

The process of revising the one-shot gives librarians an opportunity to examine both their assumptions and the knowledge that they have acquired about teaching research. Revising in a collaborative manner also leads to discussion, debate, and creative problem solving. It is a process that nurtures professional growth. But the growth doesn't end with the lesson design process: if the lesson plan that results is not a "canned" lecture, then having a classroom that encourages active learning also promotes instructional development. With every class being unique and students raising different questions, the librarian must learn to improvise, to adapt to the current class's information needs. The more librarians improvise, the more they learn about how students think about research and how best to teach them.

PLAN, COMMUNICATE, GO!

Once the deficits of the one-shot are reframed and the potential for both students and librarians considered, revising the one-shot seems more feasible. The desire for change is a real prerequisite; the next step is to plan, communicate, and implement change.

Librarians can choose to implement changes in their teaching incrementally or step-by-step. Such change offers low risk and low investment. According to Herbert Kindler, who wrote on incremental and transformational change roughly a quarter of a century ago, incremental change is effective when "the assumptions of the current system are acceptable to stakeholders."[13] Considering faculty a stakeholder, librarians can easily make changes to the way they teach without fundamentally uprooting the existing model. For faculty who are generally satisfied with the library instruction their students receive, this approach has been and continues to be pragmatic. A librarian who typically demonstrates a rehearsed search strategy to illustrate a point may, for example, introduce an element of interactivity to a class by instead asking students for search ideas. In so doing, the librarian builds his or her own confidence in a teaching situation that is more extemporaneous and less rehearsed. The faculty member is unlikely to see such changes to teaching style as challenging the agreed-upon (tacitly or explicitly) objectives of the class. As Kindler writes, such incremental changes are "intended to do more of the same but better."[14] Conscientious instruction librarians are doing this to some extent every time they teach.

Transformational, or systematic, change requires greater planning, collaboration, buy-in, and risk taking. It is necessary when incremental change is inadequate. Transformational change alters not only the activities toward a goal or objective, but the goal or objectives themselves. For example, if a desired objective of a one-shot lesson had traditionally been for students to find journal articles on their current research topics, a new goal for a transformed lesson might be the ability of students to transfer skills learned in finding journal articles for one topic to other research topics or situations. This goal may have always been an unconscious or assumed one, but articulating it will require changing the focus of the entire lesson. That, in turn, will change some things that have to happen outside of the 50-minute class time, necessitating the support and commitment of faculty. In addition to the effort required to enact it, transformational change faces additional challenges and potential resistance, which Kindler refers to as "fear of separation and fear of failure in attempting a creative leap."[15] It can be disconcerting, even somewhat frightening, to stray from the comfort of a lesson over which the librarian had total control to a model that is unpredictable and requires a greater level of engagement from other participants. What if it flops? Involving the faculty member in the change, rather than going it alone, is a strategy for minimizing risk and addressing those fears. According to change management literature, teams with shared and well-articulated goals are most effective in implementing qualitative improvements.[16] Because the revisioning of the one-shot is focused on both librarian and faculty priorities for student learning, involving a collaborative team will lead to a more robust examination of these priorities.

To enact transformational change in the library one-shot, the librarian will very likely be the one to initiate change and must take a leadership role in enacting it. In subsequent chapters we will provide strategies for identifying and articulating shared goals, through developing or fostering professional relationships with faculty, participating on campus committees, or addressing accreditation goals or other shared outcome measures.

NOTES

1. William Badke, *Teaching Research Processes: The Faculty Role in the Development of Skilled Student Researchers* (Oxford, UK: Chandos, 2012), 44–45.

2. Yvonne Mery, Jill Newby, and Ke Peng. "Why One-Shot Information Literacy Sessions Are Not the Future of Instruction: A Case for Online Credit Courses," *College & Research Libraries* 73, no. 4 (2012): 366–77, doi:10.5860/crl-271; W. Badke, "Ramping Up the One-

Shot," *Online* 33, no. 2 (2012): 47–49; Barbara Ferrer Kenney, "Revitalizing the One-Shot Instruction Session Using Problem-Based Learning," *Reference & User Services Quarterly* 47, no. 4 (2008): 386–91; Teresa M. Bean and Sabrina N. Thomas, "Being Like Both: Library Instruction Methods that Outshine the One-Shot," *Public Services Quarterly* 6 (2010): 237–49, doi:10.1080/15228959.2010.497746.

3. Julie Rabine and Catherine Cardwell, "Start Making Sense: Practical Approaches to Outcomes Assessment for Libraries," *Research Strategies* 17, no. 4 (2000): 326, doi:10.1016/S0734-3310(01)00051-9.

4. Ellen E. Damko, "Student Attitudes toward Bibliographic Instruction" (master's thesis, Kent State University, 1990).

5. Ada M. Ducas and Nicole Michaud-Oystryk, "Toward a New Enterprise: Capitalizing on the Faculty/Librarian Partnership," *College & Research Libraries* 64, no. 1 (January 2003): 58, doi:10.5860/crl.64.1.55.

6. Frank Coffield, David Moseley, Elaine Hall, and Kathryn Ecclestone, "Learning Styles and Pedagogy in Post-16 Learning: A Systematic and Critical Review" (London: Learning and Skills Research Centre, 2004), http://hdl.voced.edu.au/10707/69027.

7. Eileen E. Allen, "Active Learning and Teaching: Improving Postsecondary Library Instruction," *The Reference Librarian* no. 51/52 (1995): 89–103, doi:10.1300/J120v24n51_10.

8. Elizabeth F. Barkley, *Student Engagement Techniques: A Handbook for College Faculty* (San Francisco: Jossey-Bass, 2010), 17.

9. Paulo Freire, *Pedagogy of the Oppressed*, 30th anniv. ed., trans. Myra Bergman Ramos (New York: Continuum, 2000), 71–86.

10. National Institute of Education, *Involvement in Learning: Realizing the Potential of American Higher Education. Final Report of the Study Group on the Conditions of Excellence in American Higher Education* (Washington, DC: Government Printing Office, 1984).

11. Katherine Strober Dabbour, "Applying Active Learning Methods to the Design of Library Instruction for a Freshman Seminar," *College & Research Libraries* 58, no. 4 (1997): 299–308, doi:10.5860/crl.58.4.299.

12. Barkley, *Student Engagement Techniques*, 17.

13. Herbert S. Kindler, "Two Planning Strategies: Incremental Change and Transformational Change," *Group & Organization Studies* 4, no. 4 (1979): 477, doi:10.1177/105960117900400409.

14. Ibid., 476.

15. Ibid., 478.

16. Esther Cameron and Mike Green, *Making Sense of Change Management: A Complete Guide to the Models, Tools and Techniques of Organizational Change*, 3rd ed. (London: Kogan Page, 2012), 82.

3

Having Conversations

Beginning the Lesson Study Approach

IDENTIFYING EXISTING
STRUCTURES FOR COLLABORATION

It is one thing to get librarians on board for transformational instructional change on the one-shot; it is quite another to recruit departmental faculty, who are subject to all the regular obligations and time constraints of their positions and who may view library instruction as out of their bailiwick. To gather interest in and build momentum for this kind of change, look to existing organizational relationships, incentives, and structures that you can make use of. An institution's strategic plan may provide a vehicle for enlisting collaborators in work toward a shared goal. Likewise, institutional or departmental accreditation reviews or other assessment structures may provide incentive for partnering in the infusion of information literacy into the curriculum. Many librarians have found that when an institution is undergoing curricular redesign, such as revamping liberal education goals and outcomes, that process offers a ripe opportunity for integrating information literacy into the curriculum. It is important for librarians to be aware of and involved in these campus-wide issues to the greatest extent possible. Familiarity with shared institutional goals and initiatives enables librarians to frame information literacy concerns in terms that are understood and valued by the greater academic community.

There are organizations, such as the Association of American Colleges & Universities (AAC&U), that also help further the academic conversation about information literacy across disciplines. With more than 1,300 institutions of higher education as members, AAC&U supports and advances liberal education, defined as "a philosophy of education that empowers individuals with broad knowledge and transferable skills, and a strong sense of value, ethics, and civic engagement."[1] Through its Liberal Education and America's Promise (LEAP) program, AAC&U promotes liberal education for all students regardless of major and provides guidance for achieving and authentically assessing liberal education learning outcomes. AAC&U has developed 16 rubrics for assessing these outcomes, which are used and adapted by colleges and universities throughout the country.[2] Among these rubrics is one specifically for information literacy,[3] but among the other 15 rubrics are elements that assess information literacy concepts using different terminology. For example, the Critical Thinking VALUE Rubric defines critical thinking as "a habit of mind characterized by the comprehensive exploration of issues, ideas, artifacts, and events before accepting or formulating an opinion or conclusion."[4] It assesses a student's use of evidence, described as "selecting and using information to investigate a point of view or conclusion."[5] Similarly, the Civic Engagement VALUE Rubric assesses a student's ability to connect and extend "knowledge (facts, theories, etc.) from one's own academic study/field/discipline to civic engagement and to one's own participation in civic life, politics, and government."[6] It is important for librarians to recognize the various manifestations of information literacy concepts and to be ready to adopt the language that resonates with a particular discipline, group of educators, or administrators in building collaborations and identifying shared goals; AAC&U is one example.

Accreditation groups for disciplines can also provide guidance in ways that are particularly meaningful to collaborating departmental faculty. The American Association of Colleges of Nursing in its recommendations for baccalaureate nursing education includes nine "essentials," one of which is "scholarship for evidence-based practice." This essential, among other things, states that a student should be able to "collaborate in the collection, documentation, and dissemination of evidence, . . . evaluate the credibility of source of information, including but not limited to databases and Internet resources, . . . [and] demonstrate an understanding of the basic elements of the research process and models for applying evidence to clinical practice."[7] In collaborating with nursing faculty and administrators, the librarian would do well to frame discussions of shared information literacy concepts in terms such as "evidence-based" that reflect the vernacular of that field. The Association of College & Research Libraries (ACRL) maintains a list of information literacy standards as defined by various accrediting organizations and professional associations that can serve as a valuable resource for librarians for finding relevant standards for discipline-specific lessons.[8]

In addition to educational standards, librarians should be familiar with structures and initiatives on campus that impact curricular improvement and change. Librarians should make it their job to be involved in institutional efforts devoted to curricular redesign and support, academic policies, and assessment. One can do this by volunteering to serve on committees, attending open campus meetings, and by taking advantage of teaching and learning professional development opportunities on campus.

INTRODUCING LESSON STUDY

At our institution, the campus's Center for Excellence in Teaching and Learning (CETL) provided an effective structure upon which to initiate change. The University of Wisconsin–Eau Claire CETL was established to offer professional development opportunities and support for teaching, learning, and assessment on campus. Several years ago, CETL staff began promoting a method of instruction planning and assessment called "Lesson Study," and they were looking for faculty interested in experimenting with this model. Lesson Study is a process that involves a group (typically five to seven people) working together in the intensive planning, execution, observation, and assessment of a single lesson. Originating in Japan in the elementary school system, the Lesson Study method found its way into American K–12 schools in the late 1990s. Only recently has Lesson Study begun to catch on in higher education. The University of Wisconsin System has been notable in actively embracing the Lesson Study method. Bill Cerbin, of the University of Wisconsin–La Crosse, has been an enthusiastic supporter of incorporating the Lesson Study into higher education and, in 2011, published the first book devoted to Lesson Study in higher education.[9]

Lesson Study is an iterative process comprising five steps that can be repeated as needed (see figure 3.1). Once a Lesson Study team is formed, the group works together to achieve the following:

1. Draft goals
2. Plan the lesson
3. Teach/observe the lesson
4. Discuss and reflect on the lesson
5. Revise the lesson

The concept of Lesson Study was being actively promoted and supported on our campus. We realized that with its emphasis on a single lesson, it could be an ideal vehicle for improving the longstanding one-shot library instruction model. We approached the CETL director, explained how the unique circumstances of the one-shot library instruction session made it a good candidate for Lesson Study, and expressed interest in partnering with other faculty on campus. We didn't have trouble identifying a potential department with which to partner for a Lesson Study project. The English department was by far the most active "customer" of our library instruction services. Most faculty teaching sections of the English 110 class, Introduction to College Writing, invited librarians to meet with their students once during the semester. The curriculum in the English 110 classes varied radically from section to section. Some sections focused on persuasive writing, others on writing a research paper, some on literature, others on creative writing. It depended on the interests of the individual faculty members. Librarians provided instruction in support of the research needs of each section. As a result, the library instruction that students received varied greatly. At the time that we were looking for a Lesson Study partner, the English department was undertaking an ambitious project to revamp its English 110 curriculum. Among their goals was the development of a more standardized curriculum so students would have a more uniform experience aimed to develop in them the reading, writing, and rhetorical skills necessary to be successful in their college careers and beyond. The new curriculum emphasized rhetoric and critical thinking, and would come to include "Research and Inquiry" as one of its four goals. The CETL director made the initial contact with the English department to

Figure 3.1. The Lesson Study process. *Shevaun E. Watson et al., "Revising the 'One-Shot' through Lesson Study: Collaborating with Writing Faculty to Rebuild a Library Instruction Session," College & Research Libraries 74, no. 4 (2013): 383, fig. 1, doi:10.5860/crl12-255*

propose the idea of Lesson Study as a process for integrating library instruction into the new college writing experience. A sense of shared goals or outcomes, even if not yet articulated in the same way, a curricular redesign currently underway, and a team of English faculty committed to a collaborative process created a trifecta that would lead to the library's pilot Lesson Study.

While embarking on a collaborative project does not require a third party to co-ordinate and facilitate, it can be helpful. An advocate outside of the library can offer advantages. In our case, the CETL director was an effective advocate in negotiating a collaboration between the library and academic departments:

- As a professor who taught for many years, the CETL director could approach faculty as one of them, promoting the benefits of partnering with the library. This is more powerful than a librarian promoting the benefits of partnering with the library. It removes the potential for perceived self-interest.
- Using his role as the campus authority on teaching and learning, the CETL director was in a position to promote the collaboration in the context of over-arching institutional teaching and learning goals.

- Similarly, the CETL director offered neutral space. Meeting in CETL offices, rather than in a meeting room in the library or English department, gave no entity a "home turf advantage" and avoided a subtle sense that this was a library project or an English project.
- Conducting the Lesson Study under the auspices of CETL, participants received a small stipend for their work.
- The increasingly positive regard for both the scholarship of teaching and learning and in collaborative research, both on campus and among many disciplines in recent years, provided further incentive for faculty to become involved in such a project.

GETTING STARTED WITH LESSON STUDY

Potential group members in our case emerged because of their relationships with CETL or because of their positions, for example, Director of Composition or the Head of the Research and Instruction Department in the library. Once the CETL director established the interest of various participants, a team was formed. Ideally a Lesson Study team consists of five to seven members, each with a distinct role, interest, or reason for being on the team. Our team comprised three English faculty members, all of whom taught composition. The four librarian members of the team taught the composition library sessions, but also served as liaisons to different departments with differing academic cultures and pedagogical practices, and thus brought different perspectives to what this foundational library experience should be. The CETL director served as a facilitator. His role was to guide the participants through the Lesson Study process.

In retrospect, we found that our collaborative process was well described by the oft-cited Tuckman Model of Team Development,[10] which describes the team approach to problem solving. Recognizing this from the outset would have spared us some concern when our process felt uncomfortable, less productive, or contentious. Tuckman's model identifies the four stages of team development as normal and necessary:

- *Forming*: When the team forms, they may be unfamiliar with each other, or working with each other in a new context. Because roles in the group have not yet been fully defined or assumed, there is uncertainty about the purpose of the group and the task at hand. At this stage, members are more dependent on directive leadership, and in the case of Lesson Study, that could be an assigned facilitator.
- *Storming*: As the team begins its work, there may be some jockeying for position, consciously or unconsciously. Differences in personalities and philosophies may emerge, and group members may work through uncomfortable efforts at coming to terms with those differences. The assigned leadership role may be challenged or resisted. It is important for team members, including the facilitator, to understand that this can be an uncomfortable but normal stage.

- *Norming*: Team members settle into their roles and accept their differences. They establish group norms or accepted practices for interacting productively. A sense of cohesiveness and shared purpose emerges.
- *Performing*: The team is focused on the task. Trust is established, allowing team members to interact openly and honestly with less regard for roles or hierarchies.

We set up weekly meetings in CETL. Team members prepared themselves for the Lesson Study process by selecting, sharing, and reading about Lesson Study, information literacy in composition courses, and one-shot library instruction.[11] This preparation is especially important for the first experience with the Lesson Study process. We began with discussions about our experiences as librarians and English professors. The librarians discussed how difficult it was to meet the many expectations layered on the one-shot. The English faculty shared their experience in trying to include research instruction in their class. We all agreed that the university relied, mistakenly, on a single one-shot during English 110 to inoculate students with information literacy for their whole college career. This activity of forming the team and becoming oriented to the task and preexisting situation is illustrative of Tuckman's *forming* stage. We then set to work on step one of the Lesson Study, establishing goals.

LESSON STUDY, STEP ONE: IDENTIFY GOALS

In this stage, team members begin to identify the desired outcomes of the single lesson. It is important to note that we came to the table with our respective disciplines' definitions, outcomes, competency standards, rubrics, statements, and other tools for defining and assessing the concepts of information literacy. For example, academic librarians are guided by the ACRL *Information Literacy Competency Standards for Higher Education*[12] and/or the emerging *Framework for Information Literacy for Higher Education*[13]; writing instructors may be more familiar with the *WPA Outcomes Statement for First-Year Composition*.[14] What is important in the process of drafting shared goals is to let these documents inform and guide but not dictate desired outcomes of the lesson. As much as is possible, all members of the group should be equally vested in the articulation of the established goals.

This step of the Lesson Study brought the group to Tuckman's second stage of team development, which is *storming*. Storming involves working through both interpersonal and philosophical differences and conflicts. Group members are getting to know each other, figuring out their roles in the groups, and uncovering differences of opinion. The value in acknowledging this stage of group dynamics is to recognize that it can be messy, sometimes uncomfortable and even confrontational, but completely normal. In our Lesson Study team, members revealed differences of opinions in what should be emphasized in library instruction, in what constituted effective research, and even in what contributed to effective teaching. Members had differing communication styles. Some were verbose, others more succinct. Some were direct, others more nuanced. Some were linear thinkers, others more serpentine. As we became more familiar and thus comfortable with each other, we were better able to engage in candid discourse, and cohesiveness began to emerge. We began to value our different contributions. This is the stage that Tuckman refers to as *norming*. Together, we arrived at a list of goals for the lesson. The goals were not those set forth by ACRL or the Writing Program Administrators (WPA) or any other external group, nor did they mirror an established list of goals or outcomes. Rather they reflected the results of our lengthy, impassioned series of discussions. Unfortunately, the list was nine goals long.

Students will develop the following skills and understandings:

- an awareness of hierarchies of information
- an understanding of differences between keyword and subject heading searching
- the ability to refine searches on basis of results
- an understanding of citation chasing
- an understanding of where to go for different types of sources
- the ability to recognize and demonstrate transferability of search skills
- the ability to replicate searches
- the ability to document successful results
- the ability to access the actual source

We discussed the list of goals and what would be required to attain them, and we realized the list was unrealistic for a single lesson and would have to be winnowed.

Under the advisement of the facilitator, we decided to reduce the list to just one or two overarching goals. To ease this process, we came up with a series of options for the goals that didn't make the cut:

- Subsume them into the overarching goals. They would likely be communicated in the lesson but not explicitly taught or assessed.
- Address them through supplemental activities or learning objects that would take place outside of the lesson.
- Address them in another level of library instruction later in the curriculum.
- Abandon them.

The winnowing process required more conversation and negotiation, and team members then arrived at two overarching goals in which students will be able to do the following:

- Determine where to go to search for different types of resources.
- Recognize and demonstrate transferability of search skills.

Initially, we had allotted two weeks for the goal-setting step of the Lesson Study, but this process ended up taking five weeks, and it probably would have gone on longer were it not for the gentle and no-so-gentle prodding of the facilitator to move on. In retrospect, however, team members were united in their opinion that this phase was the most valuable step of Lesson Study. Through these conversations we gained a much clearer understanding of the information literacy needs of our students, the challenges and conditions experienced by our colleagues, and our own assumptions about what was important. Though not cognizant of it at the time, team members used these discussions to work through the Tuckman stages. Not all Lesson Study experiences will require as much time in the goal-setting phase. It will depend on factors such as how well team members already know each other and whether or not they have worked collaboratively in the past, how different their perceptions of information literacy and the desired outcomes of the project are, and how familiar they are with the Lesson Study process. Lesson Study teams are encouraged to be flexible with this stage to allow ample time for the team to gel and for meaningful discussions and decision making to unfold.

LESSON STUDY, STEP TWO: PLAN THE LESSON

With goals identified, the team enters the final Tuckman stage of *performing*, when group members have arrived at a clarity of purpose and have become accustomed to and comfortable with the structure of the group, making them ready to tackle the task at hand. It is time to plan the lesson. As with goal setting, it is not adequate to assume the work done or decisions made in another context, or in a different Lesson Study experience, are necessarily transferable to a new situation. These examples can inform and inspire, but each team should develop its own plan to address the unique demands and context of its situation.

In our Lesson Study, we were in agreement that we wanted the lesson to involve active learning, to emphasize inquiry over lecture. Each team member shared examples of teaching strategies they had tried, observed, or read about. Again, group differences emerged. Some group members were more structural in their approach, favoring detailed, unambiguous step-by-step worksheets for students to follow. Other members preferred a more free-flowing, open-ended approach to exploration. The team, now comfortable with its differing opinions, engaged in lively discussion to find common ground.

The lesson that emerged is shared here, not as a model lesson to be adopted as is by other institutions, but as an example. It is the first iteration of a lesson that we revised after the study and then many times since.

Our initial lesson plan (see appendix A) began with a brief welcome to the library, followed by a librarian demonstration of searching the catalog and a database using a sample topic. The lesson then included a segment when students would work with partners. First, students discussed their research topics with their partners, and then, using the catalog or the databases, students set about finding a relevant resource for their partner. They were to record enough information about their findings so that their partner could locate the item. A brief worksheet, itself a compromise between team members who preferred a more detailed worksheet and those who preferred none at all, walked the students through these steps. The Lesson Study team hoped that by searching their partners' topics rather than their own, students would be working toward the goal of transferability of skills. The idea was that searching on someone else's topic would disengage students from their own search topics and enable them to engage in the research process itself. They would then be able to transfer that process to their own topics. In this way, the lesson would be addressing the overarching goal of preparing students to recognize and demonstrate the transferability of search skills.

The second goal, determining where to go to search for different types of resources, would be addressed by letting the students choose where to search, that is, in the catalog or in a database, based on their partners' topics. Some of the other subsumed goals, it was hoped, could also be addressed in this activity. By documenting the source they found for their partner, students were documenting successful results and recording enough information to replicate a search. During this partner and research activity, the librarian would be assisting and observing the students in order to gather examples for a class discussion that would make up the final segment of the one-shot session.

This discussion portion was a crucial element of the lesson plan because it would allow the librarian to present other research strategies and concepts not previously demonstrated. For example, the librarian could use real student examples to talk about the selection of keywords: "See how Ashley was able to change her results by using the term graffiti rather than street art?" "Jake found the perfect article for his partner on superheroes but we don't own it in our library. He was referred to something called 'interlibrary loan.' Let's talk about what that is." "Notice how the book that Ajay found for Maria on running has a chapter on her topic of barefoot running. Sometimes you need to consider broader terms or related terms to find relevant material." The examples can be strategically selected by the librarian to address the goals and subsumed goals identified for the class.

With a detailed lesson plan in hand, the Lesson Study team is ready to move on to the next step of teaching and observing the lesson.

NOTES

1. "Liberal Education," Association of American Colleges and Universities, accessed April 25, 2014, http://aacu.org/resources/liberaleducation/.

2. "Partner Campuses," Association of American Colleges and Universities, accessed April 25, 2014, http://aacu.org/value/partner_campuses.cfm.

3. Terrel L. Rhodes, ed., *Assessing Outcomes and Improving Achievement: Tips and Tools for Using Rubrics* (Washington, DC: Association of American Colleges & Universities, 2010), 36–37.

4. Ibid., 25.

5. Ibid., 25.

6. Ibid., 43.

7. American Association of Colleges of Nursing, "The Essentials of Baccalaureate Education for Professional Nursing Practice" (working paper), accessed December 31, 2014 at http://www.aacn.nche.edu/education-resources/BaccEssentials08.pdf.

8. "Information Literacy in the Disciplines," Association of College & Research Libraries, modified April 13, 2014, http://wikis.ala.org/acrl/index.php/Information_literacy_in_the_disciplines.

9. Bill Cerbin, *Lesson Study: Using Classroom Inquiry to Improve Teaching and Learning in Higher Education* (Sterling, VA: Stylus Publishing, 2011).

10. Bruce W. Tuckman, "Developmental Sequence in Small Groups," *Psychological Bulletin* 63, no. 6 (1963): 384–99.

11. The following list does not encompass the entirety of what we read but is suggestive of the wide variety of articles that were read in preparation for working on a Lesson Study: Joy Becker et al., "A College Lesson Study in Calculus, Preliminary Report," *International Journal of Mathematical Education in Science & Technology* 39, no. 4 (2008): 491–503, doi:10.1080/00207390701867463; Linda Bilyeu, "Teachers and Librarians Collaborate in Lesson Study," *Knowledge Quest* 38, no. 2 (2009): 14–19; William Cerbin and Bryan Kopp, "Lesson Study as a Model for Building Pedagogical Knowledge and Improving Teaching," *International Journal of Teaching and Learning in Higher Education* 18, no. 3 (2006): 250–57; Sonal Chokshi and Clea Fernandez, "Challenges to Importing Japanese Lesson Study: Concerns, Misconceptions, and Nuances," *Phi Delta Kappan* 85, no. 7 (2004): 520–25; Shevon Desai, Marija Freeland, and Eric Frierson, "Lesson Study in Libraries," *College & Research Libraries News* 68, no. 5 (2007): 290–93; Van Houlson, "Getting Results from One-Shot Instruction: A Workshop for First-Year Students," *College & Undergraduate Libraries* 14, no. 1 (2007): 89–108, doi:10.1300/J106v14n01-07; Jeana Kriewaldt, "Reorienting Teaching Standards: Learning from Lesson Study," *Asia-Pacific Journal of Teacher Education* 40, no. 1 (2012): 31–41, doi: 10.1080/1359866X.2011.643761; Catherine Lewis, "What Is the Nature of Knowledge Development in Lesson Study?" *Educational Action Research* 17, no. 1 (2009): 95–110, doi: 10.1080/09650790802667477; Catherine Lewis et al., "Lesson Study Comes of Age in North America," *Phi Delta Kappan* 88, no. 4 (2006): 273–81; Naomi Robinson and Roza Leikin, "One Teacher, Two Lessons: The Lesson Study Process," *International Journal of Science & Mathematics Education* 10, no. 1 (2012): 139–61, doi:10.1007/s10763-011-9282-3; Stefan A. Smith, "Designing Collaborative Learning Experiences for Library Computer Classrooms," *College & Undergraduate Libraries* 11, no. 2 (2004): 65–84, doi:10.1300/J106v11n02_06; Claire Gatrell Stephens, "The School Librarian and Lesson Study Are Meant for Each Other!" *School Library Monthly* 27, no. 5 (2011): 42–44.

12. "Information Literacy Competency Standards for Higher Education," Association of College & Research Libraries, accessed May 5, 2014, http://www.ala.org/acrl/standards/informationliteracycompetency.

13. "Framework for Information Literacy for Higher Education," Association of College & Research Libraries, accessed May 5, 2014, http://acrl.ala.org/ilstandards.

14. "WPA Outcomes Statement for First-Year Composition," Council of Writing Program Administrators, accessed May 5, 2014, http://wpacouncil.org/positions/outcomes.html.

4

Implementing the New One-Shot

LESSON STUDY, STEP THREE: TEACH AND OBSERVE THE LESSON

After successfully setting goals and devising a lesson plan for the new one-shot, it's time to try the new lesson with a real class of students. The Lesson Study process requires careful and extensive observation of the lesson however, and team members must prepare for this stage by planning who they will teach, how they will observe, and who will do the teaching.

Clarify the Purpose of Observation

Librarians who teach may be accustomed to having their teaching observed and evaluated. However, unlike other classroom observations, the focus of the Lesson Study observation is not the teacher, but rather the students. While this distinction is not difficult to comprehend conceptually, it is recommended that the Lesson Study team acknowledge and internalize this idea, especially if the team includes individuals who may have supervisory or senior roles that put them in the position of evaluating performances of other members of the team. By designing our assessment materials deliberately, we also reinforced the idea that observation would focus on the students and the classroom dynamic rather than on the performance of the teaching librarian. We developed an "Observation Notes" form to prompt observers to take notes on details and behaviors that might usually be overlooked in a performance review but were integral to Lesson Study observation (see appendix B). For example, observers were encouraged to note things such as where the students sat and distribution by gender and race. They were prompted to take notes on signs of interest and engagement, as well as on evidence of disinterest or confusion.

33

For the teaching librarian in Lesson Study, having several observers may feel threatening or unnerving. However, it is fundamental that both the teaching librarian and the other team members understand that the results of the observation are not a reflection of the teacher but rather of the team's agreed-upon lesson design. Articulating this shared value can help to alleviate any anxiety about the observation. The librarian who teaches the team's lesson is really the conduit through whom the lesson is carried out; the success or failure of the lesson is a result of the group effort, not a reflection of the one person assigned to teach the session.

Select the Teaching Librarian

It may also be helpful to consider any internal organizational hierarchies or reporting structures and begin Lesson Study by having a senior librarian, or someone less vulnerable to any power differential, do the teaching the first time through. Our Lesson Study team included several librarians, some tenured, some not. We decided as a group that librarian performance during this "experimental" lesson not be part of any personnel review process. To further drive home this point, we decided that for our initial Lesson Study, the librarian doing the teaching would be one of the tenured librarians.

Identify Observers

The other members of the Lesson Study team should serve as observers during the session. They are most familiar with the goals of the session and are vested in the lesson. These individuals will be the ones doing subsequent revision to the lesson, so it is important that they see it unfold. That being said, there may be exceptions. If the course instructor is part of the Lesson Study team—and this is recommended—that instructor may have a more active role during the library lesson that would preclude him or her from solely participating as an observer. It is preferable to have the instructor actively engaged in the class, supporting and supplementing the librarian's work, rather than taking on the role of unobtrusive observer. The instructor will undoubtedly have observations and thoughts to share when the group reaches the stage of reflecting on what happened during the lesson, but the primary role of the instructor should remain that of instructor. The team may wish to invite an outside observer or two. Ideally, these observers would be familiar with the Lesson Study philosophy and purpose of observation. These observers, being unfamiliar with the lesson itself and unvested in the success of the lesson, can provide valuable perspectives. It is likely that they will pick up on details of the lesson and the student behaviors that will go unnoticed by those on the team.

Develop Observation Guidelines

Developing guidelines, or an observation form as we did, can help team members remember what specifics to focus on. During the observation, our form guided us to record student engagement levels. Were the students following along during the presentation or doing something else on their computers? What choices did they make when searching the catalog or database? What did they say to their partner during the partner exchange? Did their facial expressions, questions, or body language suggest that the lesson was moving too quickly or slowly for them? Did they begin searching on their own before prompted? The form allowed us to follow the lesson's progression so that observations could be organized by relative times and connected to specific sections of the lesson.

In planning the observation, be prepared to take notes on everything you can see or hear. In our session, we planned to listen to the students' discussions and pay attention to the dynamics during the paired exercise. We were interested in learning whether or not the paired discussions and searching seemed to work well: Would the students be reluctant to discuss their topics? Would their discussions remain on topic? Would one student dominate the discussion? Even though we went into the observation session with questions in mind, we knew that we couldn't predict—or even know while observing—what might turn out to be relevant or significant, so we planned to take in as many details as possible. A checklist of categories of observation can be helpful to keep your mind open to catching and recording details.

Observation Checklist

- *Spatial description*: seating arrangements, what the observer can see with relative ease. Do students sit toward the front of the room? By the door? Do they self-segregate by gender or other characteristic?
- *Engagement*: responsiveness, verbally and with body language; confusion or lack of interest; activity, both on task and off-task. Do students respond to librarian question? Laugh at jokes? Are they checking phones? Talking with neighbors? Engaging in unrelated activity on the computer? Do students ask questions or display other signs that suggest they are confused? Are they taking notes?
- *Activities*: cooperation level with peers; appropriateness of length of activity. Do the students have too much or too little time for certain activities? Do they finish the task at hand and move on to unrelated activities? Do they ask questions or engage in body language that suggests they are confused, bored, or irritated by the activity? Do they continue in one activity when the librarian instructor has moved onto the next stage of the lesson?
- *Outcomes*: results of students in-class work. Were students able to produce reasonable results? Can you observe that students are finding results that are potentially useful? Are they emailing, printing or saving search results? Are they asking questions or talking to neighbors about results? Are they asking questions to lead them toward more productive results?
- *Timing*: when observations occurred during lesson. At what time do students start fidgeting? How long does the librarian demo last? How long does a discussion last?

Because there can be so much to watch for, the team may decide to break up tasks so that some observers will be focusing on different things. This may depend on the number of observers, the size of the class, the layout of the teaching space, and more.

Consider the Teaching Space

It's hard to be unobtrusive with a team of observers. Even adding one observer to a classroom can change the dynamic of the class. To help alleviate disruption, it is recommended that teams plan ahead for the room in which the Lesson Study lesson will take place. How will members be arranged? Team members should be positioned throughout the room in order to maximize the observational area covered. This allows the team to get the broadest possible understanding of the student experience. If this is thought through ahead of time, observers can assume their positions on the day of the study with as little distraction as possible. Many classrooms are set up in such a way that it is impossible to observe students in all areas of the classroom. In our case, our Library Information Literacy Lab presented some serious obstacles in the form of several large concrete pillars that obstructed views from several positions. Because we had seven observers, we were able to mitigate the effect of the pillars, but we planned the seating out ahead of time. Ideally, observers want to be situated so that they can see what students are doing on their computers and hear at least some conversations among students.

Prepare the Students

Of course, to make the observation less disconcerting to students, it is important to prepare them. Several strangers throughout the room should not come as a surprise to them. Ideally, their instructor should let them know ahead of time that there will be observers at the library lesson. These observers, it should be explained, are there to observe the lesson. If the Lesson Study team is planning to present or publish research based on the observation, they should work with their institutional research board (IRB) to secure approval. The team will likely have to obtain informed consent from the students, and this could happen prior to the library session.

Plan for Additional Assessment Measures

The Lesson Study team may wish to supplement the observation with additional assessment measures, and, if so, this planning needs to happen prior to the session. As mentioned previously, if the team intends to publish or present results of these assessments, they will need to arrange for IRB approval. For our initial Lesson Study project, we wanted to include several supplemental assessments. For our initial Lesson Study, we planned to conduct focus-group discussions with the students immediately following the lesson. We also had students complete brief written surveys, and we collected worksheets that the students completed during the session.

Preparing the Team for Its Roles

So, with what seems like—and is—a lot of preparation for a single lesson, game day arrives. It's time to teach and observe the lesson. Our actual lesson was a combination of short demonstrations, paired exercises during which the students would work with partners, and class discussion (see appendix A). We had a worksheet on which students would take notes (see appendix C) that accompanied the lesson. The course instructor had prepared the class by letting them know about the study, obtaining informed consent, and making it clear that they were being observed but not evaluated. The instructor also let them know that the observers were there to observe rather than answer questions or participate.

The Librarian

It is worth noting that a new approach to teaching can be disconcerting for the teaching librarian, especially if she debuts this new technique with a room full of colleagues observing, let alone a class full of students. Recognizing that a new approach to teaching will require the librarian to develop new skills is a part of the process. To minimize anxiety as well as reliance on a script, the librarian should come to the session intimately familiar with the lesson plan. This will enable her to stick as closely as possible to the plan and return to it when unanticipated deviations occur.

The librarian we selected to lead the class had spent some time becoming familiar with the lesson outline and practicing what she was going to say during the demonstration portion of the lesson. It was more difficult to prepare for the discussion part of the lesson, as it was hard to predict what kind of responses she would get from the students. To inform the discussion portion, she and the course instructor planned to gather examples from what they saw as they observed as the students engaged in partner activities and searching. This way, they could gather examples that illustrated teaching points that would have been covered in a lecture or demo in a previous less student-centered approach to teaching. Rather, these lessons would be woven into the discussion portion of the lesson, bringing in the students' experiences. If students were reluctant to discuss their experiences, the librarian could draw from these observed examples to prompt participation.

The Course Instructor

The instructor whose class is involved in the Lesson Study has a role differentiated from both the observing team members and the teaching librarian; it is more of a facilitator role. The instructor prepares the class for the session and should plan to be actively engaged in the lesson during the session. The instructor's active involvement signals to the students the importance of the content. It can also put students at ease both with the teaching librarian, who may be new to them, and the room full of observers. In our lesson, it was important to have the instructor moving around the room, assisting students and gathering examples to be used in the discussion portion of the session. If the students are reluctant to participate in the discussion or other aspects of the lesson, the instructor has the authority and familiarity with the students to coax them to do so. The instructor provides additional information that the other team members do not have. She knows the students. In our Lesson Study, we had the instructor draft a seating chart during the lesson so that when we later discussed what happened in the classroom, she would know who we were talking about and, if appropriate, could share information about a student's usual behaviors or personality that might provide additional context for what we observed.

The Observers

The rest of the team, and the outside observers, came armed with the observation notes form (see appendix B) and a copy of the lesson plan outline (see appendix A), and took their positions in the predetermined spots in the room. As the class began, the challenge for the observers was to capture as many details and patterns as possible, without pausing to react or analyze what we saw and heard. Seeing what is happening on someone else's computer screen can be difficult in the best situation, and can be especially difficult depending on the classroom's setup and if the observer is trying to be inconspicuous. Observers shouldn't be afraid to move around a bit to see what is happening, but they should do so with an eye toward remaining unobtrusive in what they do. It's a fine line between hovering over a student to see his computer screen and lurking unnoticeably in the background. Observers should err on the side of being background noise. We tried not to draw attention to our presence, at times sacrificing seeing exactly what a student was doing, and instead relying on the observations we could make. For example, we were able to note that a student was changing keyword combinations but might not be able to see exactly what those keywords were. Observers should think of themselves as biologists in the wild, observing a rare species—students—and not disturbing their natural habitat. During this time, it is possible that students may ask observers questions since they see them as part of the instruction team or simply because it is easier than raising a hand to get the attention of the teacher. In those instances, the observers should document the questions, but inasmuch as it is possible without being rude, direct all questions to the course instructor or teaching librarian. To simply answer the question may make it "difficult to draw inferences about how well the lesson worked."[1]

Several of our team observers later recounted that they found it difficult to suspend a propensity to analyze what was going on and draw conclusions. But as the class progressed and we tried to keep up, we got better at objectively focusing on what was occurring before us. While it may feel alien to observe and not reflect, it is necessary for accurate and unskewed observations. The time for reflection is later in the Lesson Study process, when notes and observations are pooled, giving all team members a time to think about and reflect upon the various aspects of the lesson.

Here are sample observation notes taken by one member during a catalog demonstration:

- 4 try to click along.
- 3 are doing their own thing (fantasy baseball, unrelated searching), 2 of 3 are combining it with following Jane.
- 3 observe Jane with focused attention, with one still taking periodic notes.
- When Jane instructs "click at the top to get back to library home page," 3 followed, 2 went elsewhere, 1 kept searching catalog.

Supplemental Assessment

Observations are an integral part of Lesson Study and its focus on the student experience, but there are additional ways that you can gather data to help improve your team's lesson. One way our group did this was by conducting a focus group after the Lesson Study to see if the learning objectives were met. When conducting the focus groups, we had the teaching librarian and course instructor leave the area. The remaining observation group members conducted the focus group sessions. When we did our Lesson Study with the freshman English class, we conducted the focus group session immediately after the Lesson Study so that students could give their feedback while it was fresh in their minds. Additionally, because our Lesson Study introduced a new element that had students working with and doing research for partners, we wanted frank feedback on the partner activity. To ensure that students felt at ease in talking about this activity without worrying about offending a partner, we made sure to split partners up into different focus groups.

In addition to the focus group session, students took a short survey that asked them to assess the lesson. The change in the way that the librarians had taught—from lecture-based to active learning—was a major break from what we had traditionally done, and giving students an anonymous way to comment on the lesson was useful. Finally, we collected the worksheets that students completed in class as a way to assess the students' search capabilities to see if the goals of the class had been met: Did they demonstrate the ability to determine where to go for reliable sources? Were they able to transfer skills in searching on their partners' topics to searching on their own topics?

Gathering as much information as we did may not be practical for every team that runs a Lesson Study. We found that the most useful data came from the observers' comments and the students' comments from the focus group sessions. These two sets of data gave us views of how the students felt about the session as well as the observer's data on what the students were doing at various points in the session. Together, this helped us gain an overall sense of what worked and what needed to be changed. In addition to these useful formative assessment measures, we were cognizant that we had more work to do in developing summative outcomes-based assessment. We discuss this further in chapter 8.

LESSON STUDY, STEP FOUR: DISCUSS FINDINGS

After the lesson, the observers should write up their notes. The sooner this is done, the better, as the session will still be fresh in their minds. The teaching librarian and the course instructor won't have observation notes but are encouraged to write down notes with their own perceptions and thoughts about the session. If supplemental assessments were conducted, those data should be compiled as well. It is not necessary that the outside observers participate in the ensuing discussions, but they should submit written notes. The Lesson Study team members should plan to meet to discuss the observations and other data points the team has collected. They may wish to share written notes with team members prior to a meeting or bring them to the meeting. Either way, all team members should come to the meeting prepared to discuss their observations and to reflect on the goals and objectives set forth when planning the lesson. While the teaching librarian and the course instructor will provide feedback and commentary based on their unique roles in the lesson, the discussion should really focus on the observations of those who were documenting the student experience. Using what the team learns from the in-class observations and other data collected is an integral part of what makes Lesson Study a useful tool for developing and maximizing an instructional session.

One of the biggest surprises from our first Lesson Study was how much useful information the observers were able to collect. We all had classroom teaching experience and had a sense of what we thought the engagement level of our students had been, but, as observers, we realized that our perception when we were in front of a class was not the same as what one experiences when sitting among the students and observing. First, our sense of time was different. What felt rushed and short while teaching, especially while engaged in lecture or demo, did not feel at all so when observing. In fact, we quickly learned that what we thought was limited lecture/demo time in our lesson plan was still much too long to keep the students engaged. Similarly, being able to see from a student's perspective allowed us to notice things seemingly as mundane as the screen's too-small text size. This became apparent when we saw students squinting or asking their peers where the teacher clicked.

When looking at the results of the observations as a group, all participants need to remind themselves again that this is not an evaluation of the librarian who taught the lesson but rather an evaluation of the lesson. This is difficult. When an instructor learns that students were beginning to show signs of distraction not even four minutes into her captivating lecture, it is difficult not to take it somewhat personally. It may help alleviate some of this discomfort by couching discussion in terms of "our lesson" rather than "the librarian." For example, rather than saying, "Several students began whispering and fidgeting when Jane was demonstrating the database" the comment might be, "Several students began whispering and fidgeting after three minutes of the database demonstration part of our lesson." As was stated earlier, the observations are not meant to be a critique of the individual teacher, but rather to inform how the lesson can be improved to more effectively enable student learning.

LESSON STUDY, STEP FIVE: REVISE THE LESSON

When discussing the results of our initial observation, it didn't take long for our group to decide on the first change to be made to the lesson plan: we would shorten the demonstration segment even more and turn more time over to student exploration. What is interesting is that this experience didn't just change this lesson; it changed how this group of librarians taught all of their classes. Most importantly, the librarians realized that they need to lecture less and incorporate more active learning into their instruction sessions.

The partner activity component of our lesson plan was something that the group as a whole had wondered about: Would students like it? Would they understand why we had them working in pairs to describe their research topics to each other? Would they be able to transfer what they learned when searching for someone else's topic to their own topic? All of these questions were things that we sought to address through the observations, focus group questions, and survey. Each of the assessment methods shed light on aspects of these questions. We learned that those students who didn't like the partner activity didn't understand why they were being asked to do it. The team modified the lesson plan to include a brief explanation for doing the partner activity to its introduction. Students were told that a partner could provide another perspective on their topics and approaches for researching it. Students would also be able to take a step back from their own research to focus on the process of searching. Instead of setting students up for a "Cookie Monster" approach of rapidly and sloppily gobbling up as much information as possible on their own topics in a short amount of time, we tasked students with focusing their efforts on finding one good source for their partners. In our second iteration of the Lesson Study lesson with the composition program, we found that providing this brief rationale resulted in much more favorable reactions to the activity (see table 4.1)

Students also added numerous comments in the open-ended portion of the survey indicating that they liked the partner activity:

What I found most useful about this session was:

- Being able to work with someone else to get more feed back [sic] and other opinions on what to search for.
- Talking with a peer about my topic
- Having someone else look at my topic so I could get a different point of view and ideas of how to search differently
- Partner input

As mentioned, one of the most evident observations was how quickly students showed signs of becoming distracted or tuning out during the lecture and demonstration portions of the lesson. Originally, the team had set up the lesson to be front-loaded with a lecture/demonstration on how to search in both the library catalog and

Table 4.1.

I found that searching for a topic that was not my own was very helpful in learning how to do research.

Strongly Agree	Somewhat Agree	Somewhat Disagree	Strongly Disagree
3	22	2	2
10.3%	75.9%	6.9%	6.9%

databases. The next segment of the class period was set aside for working in pairs, and the last 5 to 10 minutes were devoted to a discussion of what worked—or didn't—in searching for books and articles. It became immediately apparent to observers that the introductory lecture/demonstration portion of the lesson was too long and that it needed to be broken up. During that time, students were fidgeting or going off on their own to begin searching on the computer. Very few were watching the librarian's demonstration of searching in the library catalog or databases. The demonstrated preference of students for hands-on time reinforced the Lesson Study group's assumptions and decision to incorporate active learning, even if this initial attempt proved inadequate.

The team had originally decided to demonstrate both search tools (library catalog and article database) at the beginning of the lesson and then let the students select from the tools to find a good source for their partners. This was intended to address one of the two stated goals for the class: *Students will be able to determine where to go to search for different types of resources.* However, in losing the interest of the students, the lesson was not effective. Observations also revealed that the discussion portion of the class seemed very effective. Students were engaged and contributing and the discussion proved to be a successful strategy for conveying content.

The team made some modifications to the lesson plan (see appendix D) to rectify the long demo problem and to better harness the value of the discussion. They decided to try breaking the lecture/demonstration portion of the class into two sections. An introduction to the class and partner activity would be followed by a brief (less than three minutes) demonstration on how to use the catalog. The students engaged in their partner discussion and went to work searching the catalog. Then the class came together for discussion on that experience. Following this discussion, the teaching librarian briefly demonstrated how to find articles in a library database, and the students set about searching again. Another discussion followed, during which students could talk about their experiences and also reflect on the differences between the different search tools and results. The worksheet (see appendix E) was updated to reflect the lesson changes.

With so much content now dependent on the discussion portion of the lesson, librarians came to realize that they would have to hone different teaching skills to make these discussions work well. While students worked in pairs or individually, the librarian would have to be on the alert for evidence and examples that could be used to facilitate a meaningful discussion. The team felt that having examples they could point to during discussion would get the students talking more; the team also believed that students would be more likely to pay attention to their peers describing effective search strategies rather than having the librarian do that.

As if to prove that the Lesson Study process is never truly over, the team has had to continue updating the lesson as the library's tools have changed. The library has since added a resource discovery layer to the library's search experience, removing the need to show students how to search for a book and article separately. Thus, the lesson plan has been whittled down further (see appendix F) to having a brief introduction and demonstration of the search tool followed by the partner activity and discussion of effective search strategies, and ending with students demonstrating a transfer of skills by finding information on their own topics.

In observing student behaviors during the partner activity, we learned that they did not want to bother with writing citation information down on worksheets for their partners and were more apt to just e-mail an article to their partners. We updated the worksheet again (see appendix G) to reflect this preference, which the team saw as more useful and efficient anyway.

The team has taught and revised the Lesson Study lesson many times, adjusting the goals, schedule, and worksheets. We have used observations, changes in technology, and new assessment feedback to further refine and improve the lesson. According to Makoto Yoshida, this process allows teachers to "discuss the lesson in a more thoughtful and systematic manner, based on actual observation of the students' learning process."[2] Additionally, as is pointed out by Jennifer Stepanek et al., teaching the lesson again "ensures that they [the instructors] immediately begin using what they learned."[3] Both of these statements hold true for the team of librarians involved in Lesson Study. Instead of relying on the perceptions of the teaching librarian alone—perceptions that Lesson Study taught us can be incomplete, inaccurate, and skewed—the team was able to gather data to make informed decisions on how best to develop a lesson used for first-year composition. Because the class was one that was taught multiple times a semester by multiple librarians, the team was able to utilize what they'd learned right away in multiple classes the following semester.

NOTES

1. Catherine C. Lewis, *Lesson Study: A Handbook of Teacher-Led Instructional Change* (Philadelphia: Research for Better Schools, 2002), 68.

2. Ibid., 43.

3. Jennifer Stepanek, et al., *Leading Lesson Study: A Practical Guide for Teachers and Facilitators* (Thousand Oaks, CA: Corwin Press, 2007), 109.

5

Expanding the Process

The Lesson Study in Other Disciplines

Successful library instruction collaborations can be like hit television shows in that they lead to spin-offs. As the first Lesson Study project was wrapping up, we began planning to bring this model to other departments and groups of instructors. While the resulting lesson of one Lesson Study is not intended to be inserted as a finished product into another course or curriculum, it can provide a starting point. After investing a great deal of time, discussion, and reflection in our initial Lesson Study, our librarians had gained a much better understanding of what our faculty want their students to know about information literacy and research skills. Equally important, by starting with the first-year composition class, a foundational course through which almost all students will pass, we had established a baseline of what all students at the university should know by the end of their first year. This provided an opportunity for librarians and faculty to build on previous knowledge when creating instruction sessions for upper level students. In the past, librarians could assume no prior knowledge, as some students may not have been exposed to library instruction in their first-year composition course. As a result, librarians had to start at the beginning with each class and rarely had time to progress much beyond that. As you will see in the two examples described in this chapter, Lesson Study collaborations enabled the one-shot instruction sessions to move from being repeats to becoming a series of scaffolded lessons. The next two collaborations paired librarians with faculty in the sciences and in nursing.

LESSON STUDY IN THE SCIENCES: INTRODUCTION AND GOAL SETTING

Encouraged by the results of the library and English department Lesson Study collaboration, the Center for Excellence in Teaching and Learning (CETL) director, who served as the facilitator, suggested another collaboration. He approached the library's liaison to the sciences in order to gauge his interest in involvement in a new Lesson Study.

Believing the experience that we had with the English department Lesson Study was a process that could be replicated in other disciplines, the CETL director invited faculty in the sciences (biology, physics, chemistry, and geography) to be part of a new Lesson Study. Biology faculty had conducted a prior Lesson Study of their own, so they were familiar with the process and its utility.

After getting agreement from disciplinary faculty and librarian, the team of faculty set forth on making a new lesson using the Lesson Study methodology. It was beneficial to have both the librarian and CETL director as part of this group, as they were involved in the most recent Lesson Study with the first-year composition program—the librarian as a team member and the director as facilitator. The CETL director had also facilitated an earlier biology Lesson Study, which was a little different in that it did not feature a collaboration between the library and disciplinary faculty. These prior experiences helped make it easier to "sell" the Lesson Study methodology to skeptical faculty who might otherwise question the seemingly excessive investment of time on a single lesson. The new science Lesson Study would build on the baseline information literacy instruction provided in the first-year composition course. The librarian and the facilitator could now describe to science faculty the information literacy concepts that students emerging from their first year should have been introduced to. Library instruction in the disciplinary science courses could then assume prior exposure and build on it. Additionally, the initial steps of Lesson Study (goal setting, planning the lesson) were much easier to get through because of the two experienced members; they gave examples of prior successful Lesson Study goals, outcomes, and teaching strategies that could be modified to meet the needs of a new class.

The CETL director and librarian explained the purpose of the new standardized first-year composition program, which included the library lesson developed through the Lesson Study project, detailing the level of library instruction that students received. It became apparent that science faculty assumed a much greater level of preparedness on the part of the students coming into their classes. They hadn't really thought about it but assumed that students were learning a great deal more research instruction than is feasible in a one-shot lesson. The misperception that *everything* was covered and that students emerged from a first-year composition course knowledgeable about the myriad ways in which to search, find, evaluate, and synthesize sources of information was a relic of how librarians had taught one-shot classes in the past. Even though the librarians and English faculty involved in the initial Lesson Study had struggled with and worked through these unrealistic expectations and promises, there was still an entire campus of faculty who had not and still held those inaccurate perceptions. Even after learning about the first-year composition Lesson Study discussions and outcomes, the science faculty didn't fully comprehend the complex nature of the information literacy concepts that students needed to learn and how it could be that they hadn't already learned them in their first-year composition class. After all, isn't that where this sort of learning is supposed to take place? Should science faculty have to devote their teaching time to information literacy instruction when they have so much else to cover? To give the science faculty a better sense of what content could actually be covered in the first-year composition one-shot library session, the librarian taught the science faculty members as if they were the students in the class. This was an eye-opening experience for the faculty. They learned things about the library that they didn't know and that had recently changed, and they came away with a better understanding of what students actually know when they come to college and how much there is for them to learn. And they began to understand how it was unrealistic to think that these concepts could be taught in a single 50-minute session once in a student's college career. The faculty emerged from this demonstration with a clearer understanding of their students' preparedness, making it possible for the group to move forward with creating realistic goals that would build on this experience.

The development of the science Lesson Study took place during one summer with the group meeting weekly for approximately two hours each time. With so many different disciplines represented, the group decided to pick one discipline for which it would design a lesson. This lesson would have to be easily adaptable so that it could work with the other science disciplines with minimal revision. Faculty members in each discipline discussed what they saw from their students in terms of writing and research skills. Not surprisingly, many observed deficiencies were the same across disciplines, building confidence among the faculty that the lesson developed for a class other than their own would be relevant to the needs of their students as well. In the end, the group opted to create a lesson for chemistry students who were on campus over the summer doing research with some of this Lesson Study's faculty.

Having selected the "class" of chemistry students as their test group, the Lesson Study team needed to decide on what they wanted to accomplish. After much deliberation and negotiation, the group arrived at six goals for the lesson. Six goals may sound overly ambitious, especially considering that the English composition Lesson Study identified just two goals as being attainable. However, some were straightforward task-based goals, making them simpler to convey than the more conceptual goals. See table 5.1.

PLANNING, DEVELOPING, AND
TEACHING THE LESSON STUDY IN THE SCIENCES

In order to address all goals, the team also decided to develop several "prerequisite" activities to prepare students for the library one-shot lesson. A common concern among the science faculty was that their students had trouble identifying what constituted a "good" journal or database. They wanted the librarian to cover that in the lesson. Upon further discussion of what this actually means, it was decided that introducing students to credible and valued publications in the discipline would be

Table 5.1.

Goal	Description
Find and select a database	The students were introduced to the array of databases for chemistry.
Conduct a search	Students searched the Web of Science (WoS) database, using appropriate keywords and phrases to find needed information.
Refine a search	Students think of ways within the database to improve their search using things like subject headings, limits, and other options.
Select an article	Students were to look at various attributes within WoS, such as times cited, abstract, title, whether it was a research article, etc., to determine its utility for their research question.
Use EndNote to save the reference to the article	Students would save their research results so that they could retrieve them later and create bibliographies for their research.
Get the full text of the article	Students would secure articles in print or online, or request from another library as needed.

a more effective lesson coming from the faculty, who are the ultimate subject experts in their fields, rather than from the librarian. Librarians have expertise, to be sure, but not necessarily the subject expertise of the faculty. And they often have not had the opportunity to earn from the students a comparable level of credence or authority as that held by disciplinary faculty. The group decided to address this issue and others in a prerequisite activity (see appendix H). They created a handout, which the students would get before the lesson, with specific objectives so that students could be prepared for the class session. The purpose of the handout was to ensure that the professor would cover the following before the Lesson Study session:

1. Describe hierarchies of information in his/her field of study. (What journals/databases do the faculty use in their own research?)
2. Explain what type of information the students should search for (primary, secondary, review, peer review, editorial, etc.) and how to distinguish these different types of articles from one another.
3. Introduce EndNote as a tool to help organize and store research results and have the students create an account.
4. Make sure the students have prepared a list of keywords to use in searching their research topic. To fulfill this step, students would meet with their faculty researcher and talk about their topic so that they could learn some of the terminology.

After creating the handout and making sure that students had enough prerequisite information to complete the lesson, the group began developing the instructional session itself. With the goals in mind, the group created a worksheet (see appendix I) that would be completed in class by students. One of the key components of the worksheet was that students were to write down the steps that they took to get to their selected article so that the search could be replicated and to aid in recall. As Bohay, Blakely, Tamplin, and Radavansky describe in their study on note taking, "Performance improved when people more actively engage with the information, such as by taking notes. . . . This increased engagement . . . allowed people to more accurately respond to subsequent memory test questions."[1] The Lesson Study group postulated that although completing a worksheet is not necessarily analogous to note taking, having the students write down their library research steps would help them remember specific methods that were effective when searching for and locating information.

The class would be taught by a librarian in a standard 50-minute one-shot style. Teaching the session was done in an active-learning manner consistent with the previous lesson developed through the first-year composition Lesson Study: the librarian gave a brief introduction to what the students needed to do and set them free to actively engage with the tools and the worksheet. The librarian helped individual students as needed and facilitated discussion, interspersing questions and explanations throughout the lesson.

EVALUATING AND REFINING THE LESSON STUDY IN THE SCIENCES

At the conclusion of the lesson, the librarian photocopied the worksheets to further understand students' comprehension of the lesson's goals and asked students to complete a short (eight questions) feedback form that would provide quantifiable data to get the student perspective on the lesson. One of the most striking results from the feedback form indicated that 100 percent of students felt that they were successful in their searching for and selecting an article. However, the librarian was only able to reproduce their search 38 percent of the time based on the students' documented steps.

In discussing these implications, Lesson Study faculty felt that they needed to place more emphasis on the importance of creating a written record of search strategies and results. They wanted to revise the lesson in a way that would encourage students to be more accountable in documenting their searches. To that end, the group decided to have students give their documented search steps to another student, who would attempt to repeat the search. The student replicating the search would complete the worksheet, indicating if the search worked and providing any additional comments. The students would then discuss any questions or issues that arose from this process. Interestingly, in the previous first-year composition Lesson Study, the idea of completing a worksheet detailing the steps of a search was immediately eschewed. English faculty and some librarians in that group viewed such an activity as tedious and unnecessary busywork with the potential to inhibit the nonlinear exploratory nature of research. Written worksheets and assignments are not advisable or even appropriate in all disciplines. However, in the sciences, tracking the details of a process so that results can be replicated is extremely important. For this particular Lesson Study, the team felt it was a good way to model this practice on the worksheet. Becoming cognizant of the partner department's culture is extremely important for a successful cross-departmental collaboration.

One of the most important observations noted by the faculty observers during the science Lesson Study session was a perception that the students accorded the librarian less authority than the teaching faculty. In order to rectify this situation, the faculty member needed to be more engaged in the class session itself, asking questions or clarifying and emphasizing points that the librarian was making in order to "endorse" the librarian and make it clear to students that the librarian and faculty were in close collaboration on this class.

The lesson developed through this Lesson Study continues to be taught in chemistry and geography classes, and a revised version of the lesson is being used with physics classes. Other science faculty who were not involved with the Lesson Study have heard from their peers about the lesson and have asked for it to be taught in their classes as well. In fact, Lesson Study team members were encouraged by the CETL director to talk to their peers about the lesson and the experience. A recommendation from other faculty is one of the most effective promotional devices for library instruction.

SCAFFOLDING INFORMATION LITERACY ACROSS A CURRICULUM: LESSON STUDY IN NURSING

After successful Lesson Study collaborations between the library and disciplinary faculty, the CETL director continued to look for opportunities to match the needs of disciplinary faculty with the pedagogical improvement method of Lesson Study. As it happened, one presented itself shortly after completion of the science Lesson Study: the College of Nursing was interested.

Selling the nursing faculty on the concept of Lesson Study was not terribly difficult for a few reasons. First, our institution's faculty in nursing have a history of seeking professional-development help through CETL. Second, several nursing faculty were seeking ways to improve the teaching of specific nursing skills and concepts that aligned with information literacy outcomes. Perhaps most importantly, as a service profession, faculty members in nursing are by nature very collaborative and appreciate working with others to improve their practice.

In discussing their pedagogical needs, the nursing faculty emphasized their commitment to integrating evidence-based practice into the curriculum. As they discussed evidence-based practice, the CETL director—having by this time been well-schooled in information literacy concepts—recognized it as information literacy by another name. He saw collaboration with the library as a natural fit. A team was

formed comprising three nursing faculty and three librarians, including the liaison
to nursing as well as two librarians who had experience working with the College of
Nursing and with the Lesson Study process. Continuing to reflect upon and refine
a lesson are key components of the Lesson Study process. Because two librarians
could draw upon their previous experiences of designing a lesson with the first-year
composition team and reflect upon what worked well and what didn't, this new team
was able to use that experience to jump-start a Lesson Study in nursing. They were
able to bring in some of the goals from previous Lesson Studies as a starting point
for discussion about what the goals for the nursing Lesson Study should be. Materials
from the previous Lesson Studies (worksheets, feedback forms, observation sheets,
focus group questions, etc.) could be shared, considered, and adapted for the new
Lesson Study.

While starting the nursing Lesson Study was made easier by having experienced
members as part of the team, it should be noted that it is vitally important for
each Lesson Study team to work through all steps in the Lesson Study process. It
is this process that enables group members to get to know each other, articulate
and understand the issues, and develop a common language that resonates within
their respective disciplines. Within the nursing discipline, for example, there is an
external push from accrediting agencies and professional organizations to incorporate evidence-based practice into the curriculum so that future nurses can better
apply those concepts to improve patient outcomes.[2] One of the major components
of evidence-based practice is the ability to find and use high-quality information
effectively. Librarians refer to those same concepts as information literacy. It was
through the stages of Lesson Study that the nurses and librarians were able to
identify the intersection of their goals and share their respective discipline's approaches, challenges, and terminology. As was stated in chapter 3, the initial stage
of Lesson Study helped this team come together and forge bonds. Experience with
a number of Lesson Studies shows us that this step is crucial to making Lesson
Study successful.

When the group met to address the goals of the collaboration, it became apparent
very quickly to the experienced Lesson Study team members that what the nursing
faculty wanted—students to be able to find, access, evaluate, and use evidence-based
practice resources—could not be reasonably accomplished in one lesson. The librarians' experiences with the first-year composition Lesson Study helped immensely
as they were able to describe the process of sifting and winnowing from nine goals
to two that they felt could be reasonably accomplished in one 50-minute session.
Though Lesson Study traditionally looks at a single lesson, the group agreed that
what they wanted was more than what could or should be done in one 50-minute
session. Instead, the team would plan a series of lessons, each of which would be
developed using the Lesson Study methodology.

The project expanded traditional Lesson Study concepts by focusing not just on
a single session in a single class but rather on a series of lessons integrated into an
entire curriculum. As the concept expanded, it became clear that the lessons would

be developed and integrated progressively over a period of three years. That way each Lesson Study instruction session would be incorporated into the curriculum when appropriate. Because students in the nursing program enter as sophomores, the integration would happen in the sophomore, junior, and senior years. The nursing faculty in the Lesson Study group taught a class at each of the three levels, which the group felt would allow for a scaffolded or tiered instruction curriculum.

A scaffolded integration of multiple lesson studies requires a lot of coordination. Thus, a group embarking on a curriculum-wide series of Lesson Studies must invest more time in goal setting and planning. In our case, the entire three-year program had to be mapped out before the first lesson could be developed and taught. The team also planned more robust methods of assessment to evaluate this ambitious project. Assessment included a longitudinal analysis of student learning and retention, and compared data of students in the Lesson Study cohort to that of a control group of students who hadn't had any of the nursing Lesson Study interventions.

This set of lessons continued to build on the experience of previous Lesson Studies. Nurses expressed frustration that their students didn't understand the distinctions between different types of literature. Similar to the concern expressed by faculty in the science Lesson Study, nursing faculty were frustrated that students often used opinion pieces and letters to the editor inappropriately, unable to distinguish them from research articles. Their students struggled with identifying sources that meet the standards for the highest-quality evidence, as is required within evidence-based practice. The librarian who had been involved in the science Lesson Study suggested borrowing from the prerequisite exercises developed for the science Lesson Study. This prerequisite exercise was reworked for the nursing curriculum (see appendix J) and formed the basis for the series of library interventions that followed.

Table 5.2 outlines the overarching goal of this curricular Lesson Study as well as the goals for individual library sessions in the three-year progression.

Table 5.2.   Goals of Nursing Lesson Studies

Entire study	Students will be able to retrieve various levels of scholarly information and apply or evaluate their usefulness to clinical practice.
Sophomore (prerequisite) intervention	The student will demonstrate an understanding of nursing information structure and literature.
Sophomore intervention	The student will demonstrate effective search strategies to retrieve one scholarly piece of evidence from CINAHL to support their clinical PICO question.
Junior intervention	The student will be able to demonstrate advanced search strategies to select high-quality pieces of evidence to support their clinical PICO question.
Senior intervention	The student will be able to demonstrate using "best practice" evidence to evaluate nursing practice within the clinical setting.

Sophomore Intervention

The lesson developed for the sophomore students centered on a "PICO" question. PICO is a mnemonic commonly used in the medical field to convert a clinical scenario into an answerable, well-built clinical question. It identifies four components:

1. Population
2. Intervention
3. Control/comparison
4. Outcome

A health-care professional doing training for first responders may have to decide whether to teach compression-only cardiopulmonary resuscitation (CPR) or traditional CPR. To make this determination, they would want to know which one offers the better chance of survival. This might be a PICO question derived from this scenario:

In people receiving cardiopulmonary resuscitation (CPR), how does compression-only CPR compare with traditional CPR in terms of survival rate?

(P)opulation: All patients receiving CPR

(I)ntervention: Compression-only CPR

(C)ontrol: Traditional CPR

(O)utcome: Survival rates

The students in the sophomore class worked in groups to develop their own PICO questions in preparation for the first library session. At the start of the session, students were given a handout that served both as a resource and as a worksheet for the interactive exercise during the session (see appendix K). Librarians began the session by using a sample PICO question described on the handout to generate search terms. They then conducted a search in the Cumulative Index to Nursing and Allied Health Literature (CINAHL) database and briefly demonstrated the use of limits and other techniques for refining a search in retrieving a scholarly piece of evidence for the PICO question. Working in groups, students mirrored this process with their own PICO question and recorded the process on their worksheet. While students completed the worksheet, the librarian and nursing faculty member moved around the room, observing and providing assistance. Borrowing from previous Lesson Study lessons, the session concluded with an interactive discussion on the students' experience with the activity, emphasizing how students found and accessed their scholarly piece of evidence and addressed common problems that the students encountered or the instructors observed.

Junior Intervention

The second lesson occurred during the junior year and built on what was done in the sophomore-level session. Students again came to class with a new PICO question. Students worked in groups again to complete another worksheet (see appendix L). This time, the students searched for pieces of evidence in a number of different databases in addition to CINAHL, such as PsycINFO, MEDLINE, Nursing Reference Center, and Mosby's Nursing Consult. When the library attained a resource discovery tool (ExLibris's PRIMO) that searched across platforms and information format types, this was added to the mix. Students were charged with finding scholarly evidence that was

- published in the last seven years,
- primary research, and
- authored by a nurse.

Then students compared the search experience and the quality of their results attained from the various search tools. Finally, the class discussed the pros and cons of the tools in terms of their value to researching and answering their PICO questions.

Senior Intervention

The senior class session was designed to help students transition from their academic life to the workplace. Recognizing that senior students would soon graduate and enter workplace settings with varying access to information resources, this culminating session focused on finding evidence-based practice resources when access to traditional library resources is limited. In groups, students created another PICO question, this time derived from their field experience. Students again completed a worksheet (see appendix M) requiring them to search databases that are freely available to the public (PubMed, National Guideline Clearinghouse, MedlinePlus) in order to retrieve "best practice" evidence applicable to their PICO questions. The students, course instructor, and librarian then discussed the advantages and disadvantages of using these resources to inform clinical practice.

At every step in the process, the team worked to assess each Lesson Study plan as developed by the group. In addition to the traditional information collected through observation in a Lesson Study, the group conducted additional assessments including a pretest, questions embedded at each level in the students' exams, and a posttest. The posttest was also administered to a control group of senior students who had not had any of the Lesson Study intervention. From these data, we were able to assess each individual intervention as well as the entire series of Lesson Study interventions, comparing outcomes of students in the Lesson Study cohort to those in the traditional one-shot interventions used in the nursing program. These data also gave the nursing faculty feedback on student learning of concepts related to evidence-based practice.

The results collected showed great improvement in some areas after interventions had taken place, but they also showed that throughout the entire project some of these gains were only temporary. For example, quantitative data gathered showed that students had a pretty good understanding of the purpose of scholarly literature and, that after the sophomore level intervention, they demonstrated an ability to discern among types of articles in selecting sources. However, data gathered later in the three-year program demonstrated that they lost some proficiency in discerning among types of articles (a research study, an opinion piece, etc.) or determining how articles can be used in clinical or research practice. As a result, revisions of the lessons will include repeated emphasis on using varying types of literature throughout the curriculum, not just in the sophomore class. Qualitative data gathered provided a different prism through which the team could assess the lesson study. As students reflected on the library interventions during focus group discussions, they recognized—with some astonishment—the progressive nature of library lessons throughout the three years. Other students, as if scripted by librarians, stated that the Lesson Study interventions aided in the development of critical thinking skills. Even though the project ended after four years (inclusive of preparatory time), all library and nursing Lesson Study faculty involved came away with a greater appreciation of the intentional integration of information literacy and evidence-based practice, and are committed to continuing to work together to improve instruction for nursing students.

NEW CURRICULUM IN NURSING

Just as the Lesson Study team was wrapping up its multiyear Lesson Study project, the nursing department began redesigning its curriculum. The redesign is a phased implementation in which those entering the program as sophomores will be part of the new curriculum, while those who have already taken classes in the program will continue to receive instruction as part of the old curriculum until they graduate.

The Lesson Study interventions that the team developed are still being taught, but with changes in pedagogy, instructors, and curriculum coming, the lessons will need to be redeveloped. Fortunately, as a result of the Lesson Study process, the nursing faculty now see librarians as part of the redesign process and library instruction as an integral part of the curriculum.

BUILDING ON THE FIRST-YEAR
ONE-SHOT: CONCLUSION

Both of the discipline-specific Lesson Study projects—the one-shot science lesson and the curriculum-wide, multiple-session nursing project—built on the foundational first-year composition lesson, illustrating how a one-shot doesn't have to be the same shot every time; one shot can lead to another and then another. Without necessarily adding more librarian time in classrooms—a concern for libraries with limited staffing and resources—strategically scaffolding library one-shot sessions enables librarians to work smarter by providing a framework for building on previous knowledge rather than starting at the beginning with every meeting of students. The one-shot lesson that eventually became part of the first-year composition program taken by all students not only provided them with an information literacy foundation upon which to build; it also made the process of building subsequent information literacy instruction sessions more efficient and streamlined. It did this in two ways:

1. Librarians were able to articulate to faculty in the disciplines exactly what instruction their students received in the first year.
2. Faculty gained a better understanding of where the gaps in their students' information literacy competencies were.

The Blugold Seminar lesson—the result of the first Lesson Study—has become the foundation for all library instruction. As discussed in this chapter, it has enabled librarians to work with faculty in other disciplines through subsequent Lesson Study projects to expand information literacy instruction that students receive throughout their college careers. But it has also benefited departments and classes that have not gone through the Lesson Study process with the library. Given their experience in the Blugold Seminar, librarians are more likely to incorporate active-learning techniques into other classes and are becoming more adept at it. Similarly, knowing what students get in the Blugold Seminar allows librarians to assume prior knowledge and build upon that when they meet with upper-level classes. Finally, the Lesson Study projects have given librarians more experience and confidence in their conversations with faculty, making them better equipped to share ideas about what the library can and cannot do, and offering solid examples to encourage future collaborations with other departments.

NOTES

1. Mark Bohay et al., "Note Taking, Review, Memory, and Comprehension," *American Journal of Psychology* 124, no. 1 (2011): 71, accessed December 31, 2014, http://www.jstor.org/stable/10.5406/amerjpsyc.124.1.0063.

2. Angie Stombaugh et al., "Using Lesson Study to Integrate Information Literacy Throughout the Curriculum," *Nurse Educator* 38, no. 4 (2013): 173–77, doi:10.1097/NNE.0b013e318296db56.

6

Supplementing the One-Shot

The one-shot lesson is not the only shot of information literacy that students get. Ideally, the ideas and concepts are scaffolded and reiterated during students' courses as well as throughout their academic careers. At institutions where the one-shot library lesson is the model, it is likely due in part to library staffing and resource limitations. As a result, a sustained program will require that some information literacy instruction be done by the course instructors themselves. The librarian can develop supplemental lessons and materials and provide support for instructors in implementing them.

Librarians must be intentional in the development of this support, carefully considering goals and objectives, selecting appropriate formats, and taking steps to maximize faculty adoption of the content.

IDENTIFY GOALS AND OBJECTIVES

Work in Consultation with Faculty

In deciding what objectives to focus on first, it is best to work in consultation with faculty. The objectives may be a by-product of the Lesson Study or other library lesson collaboration, or they may arise from otherwise stated or identified needs. We have discussed goal setting for the one-shot lesson. In that process, goals and objectives are enumerated that are important but that don't fit into the session. Identify those additional goals and objectives, as they can form the basis for the array of supplementary materials you offer. In our initial Lesson Study, our lesson focused on search strategies, specifically the goals of determining where to search for different types of resources and transfering search skills from one situation to another. The goals that remained could be resolved into a list of skills and concepts, as shown in table 6.1.

Table 6.1.

Skills	*Concepts*
Concept mapping	Research as a responsive process
Citation chasing	The information cycle
Citation management	Source types
Citation style	Credibility/evaluation
Research management	Ethical use of information
	Troubleshooting research

These remaining skills and concepts became the content of supplementary lessons, activities, videos, and learning objects developed by librarians and offered to instructors to supplement their library lesson. We referred to these supplementary materials as "extras." They were all agreed upon by the Lesson Study team of librarians and instructors.

Limit Objectives Per "Extra"

The temptation to have students work toward too many objectives in one learning experience is certainly there, but there are practical considerations for resisting the impulse to compound multiple goals into one lesson or create an übertutorial.

First, it is likely that faculty will be working the learning experiences we provide into an already-crowded semester schedule. Being able to interleave information literacy lessons at the moments in which they are most relevant is an important factor. Creating a menu of "extras" that can be moved, combined, reused, and inserted in a variety of courses and curricula argues in favor of keeping them brief and built around a single objective.

Make "Extras" Developmentally and Course Appropriate

It is important that supplementary lessons recommended to faculty are both relevant to the course and appropriate for the students at that level. For example, while we knew first-year students would need to develop a system for managing the various files and resources they discovered during their exploration process, we were ambivalent as to whether learning to use a bibliographic management tool, such as EndNote, would be appropriate or helpful at the freshman level. In the end, we decided that EndNote was more helpful when students began referring to a more consistent body of sources, such as when they began research in their majors. Learning objects and lessons offering that level of instruction were not emphasized in the first-year composition course but rather in subsequent research-intensive courses.

CHOOSE A FORMAT

When developing learning experiences, an important criterion for which format to choose is how adaptable the lesson will be for individual faculty, and here we mean not just the content, but the kinds of deliverables faculty can request from students. We were concerned when considering any of the formats available for our "extras" about the advantages and disadvantages of the modes of delivery. Videos and Lib-Guides have the clear advantage of being easily deployed in or out of class, through content management systems (CMS), and via e-mail; however, they represent what is often experienced as a passive learning opportunity. We tried to mitigate this by keeping them short and pairing them with particular assignments we knew the faculty would deploy. So, for example, for our video on "concept mapping," students knew they would be using the practices described in our film immediately for class.[1] Another common recommendation is to pair videos with quizzes or post hoc assessments. We were reticent to layer these on top of the work students would already be doing with the content, not only for pedagogical reasons, but also in the interest of not creating more work for the faculty.

APPEAL TO AUDIENCE

The digital environment lends itself to the development of "extras," so looking to the literature to find advice for planning and creating digital "extras" is a good first step. The best practices commonly cited in the realm of authoring digital learning objects are heavily focused on pedagogical concerns. Some recommendations include making the objectives of the lesson clear from the outset, offering multiple experiences that cater to different learning styles, and providing some amount of active learning through the deployment of interactive exercises or quizzes. Other recommendations related to audience reception, such as keeping videos short and avoiding a dizzying array of cuts and zooms, are also common.[2] What is less common are best practices that deal with audience analysis. Perhaps there is a reluctance to draw upon the expertise of marketers and "Mad Men," but there is little discussion about how to appeal to the attention of the college-going audience. Some presumption can be made that students will be held accountable for at least engaging with assigned learning objects through assessment, but if librarians have the broader goal of creating *effective* learning objects, then considerations such as appeal to the audience need to be factored in. While libraries have neither the budgets nor the staffing for the kind of marketing analysis done by commercial publishers of learning objects, it would be helpful to import some of their practices and processes. Still, even rudimentary attempts at audience analysis can be useful. What other media do students partake in? What assumptions do they bring to the table? What topics and events resonate with them? What visual and textual rhetoric would they find insulting or juvenile? What level of intellectual challenge are they ready for? An excellent strategy for answering these questions is to include students in the development process. Student library assistants may be available to help with this process. On many campuses there is funding or course credit to support student-faculty collaborative projects, and these avenues may be options for librarians to work with student collaborators.

SHORTER IS BETTER

Another consideration emerges from the best practices surrounding digital learning objects, particularly videos: shorter is better. Most of our skill-centered videos clock in at less than three minutes, leaving little space for more than one objective. As with most best practices, this is not a hard-and-fast rule. But if you decide to make longer videos, do so intentionally. We did create one longer video—a version of the Information Cycle (see figures 6.1 and 6.2), which was inspired by Penn State's original flash video from 2004.[3] As a concept, the Information Cycle is already complex, introducing a sense of chronology to the types of sources created in response to an exigency. To better support the newly revised writing curriculum, faculty asked that our learning object also address how speakers and writers who appear later in the Information Cycle for a topic respond to earlier sources. Thusly, the video underlines a core rhetorical concept from the class: James Herrick's claim that "rhetoric is responsive."[4] This longer and more complex video is still a viable learning experience because most of the faculty show it in class and the concept of the Information Cycle is included in their text, in class discussions, and in project assignments throughout the second half of the semester.

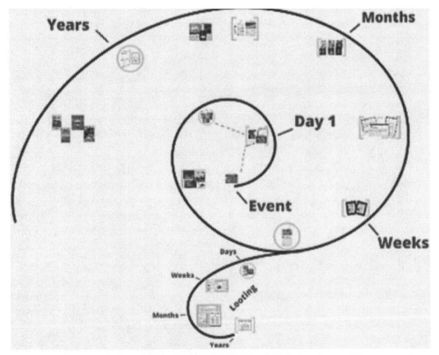

Figure 6.1. The UW–Eau Claire Information Cycle that shows how an event can have other events spin off the main story and create their own information cycles.

Figure 6.2. The UW–Eau Claire Information Cycle video traced the rhetorical shifts present in the information cycle, including the shift from summative reporting to longer, more analytical essays found in magazines like those in this image.

MAKE IT FLEXIBLE AND REUSABLE

We soon began to value digital lessons that were easily recyclable into updated versions or new lessons altogether. One of the downsides of video is that repurposing or updating it usually requires starting from scratch. For some of our shorter videos shot live or with Camtasia, this was a less daunting task. The relatively low development costs and time demands make it possible to replace videos as needed. Our Information Cycle video was a more time- and resource-intensive production, requiring sound tracks layered with Audacity and carefully timed with a Camtasia recording of a Prezi that we developed over the course of a month. The opportunity to amend or update it will have to wait until the need is glaring and we have enough time.

Using web apps, such as Storify and Scoop.it (see figure 6.3), to share curated content paired with a lesson plan offers an inexpensive and easy format that is both adaptable and recyclable. Other web apps, such as mapping software like Coggle and Lucidchart, offer platforms for students to do pre-research concept mapping and project self-assessments. Our evaluation exercise "Who Do You Trust?" (see figure 6.4), developed on Storify, allows faculty to swap out examples and customize them according to their sections' theme.

When we selected web apps for learning experiences, we looked for ones that were either already familiar to students or were known for their intuitive interface. For example, in the case of Lucidchart, we discovered that it only took a one-minute demonstration to allow students to accomplish the lesson objectives. Perhaps more impor-

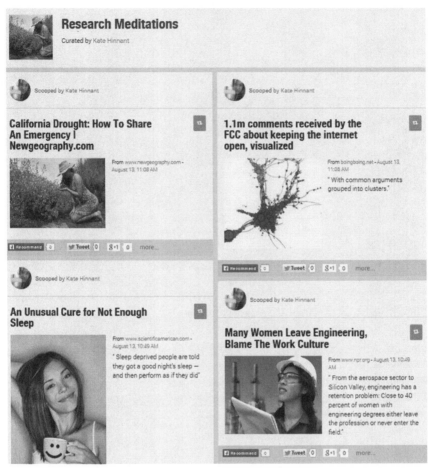

Figure 6.3.   Content curated within Scoop.it is used for low-stakes inquiry practice: students select an article of interest to them and explore the questions it raises, as well as how they think they might begin to answer those questions. For full website, see http://www.scoop.it/t/research-meditations.

tantly, faculty who have adopted Lucidchart in their classes have been able to learn it independently. In addition to freely available web apps, we also used Springshare's Lib-Guides for assignment-based library lessons, including one on background research.

The more dynamic, interactive lessons we created using web apps have several advantages in terms of mode of delivery. One is that the instructor can reinforce their relevancy during class discussion. Also, they can be tailored to the specific work students are doing on their projects. Finally, they call on students to draw upon their own experiences to learn the skills or concepts in an active way. But they also have drawbacks: they can take up entire class periods, and faculty need more support in implementing them. We have found that when the objective of a given lesson is important enough to faculty, they are more likely to turn over an entire class period to it.

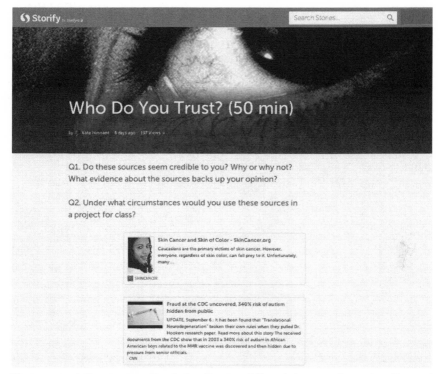

Figure 6.4. Who Do You Trust? Storify. For full website, see https://storify.com/Naranjadia/who-do-you-trust-1.

FACULTY ADOPTION OF SUPPLEMENTARY MATERIALS

Ultimately, the success of supplementary materials will depend on faculty adoption of them. Librarians can develop them with faculty input, promote them to faculty, and even develop them at the request of faculty, but there is no guarantee that faculty will use them. A variety of constraints can nullify the efforts to promote adoption of the "extras." The foremost of these is time: not all faculty plan ahead to fit this instruction into their class. Despite best intentions, some faculty cannot find space in overcrowded courses to squeeze it in. There are some steps librarians can take to maximize faculty buy-in and commitment to using the "extras."

Cultivate Advocates

When we began developing "extras," we started with the prerequisites that the Lesson Study team had determined were mandatory for the success of the students. Librarians and English faculty on the team were committed to the prerequisites—mandatory lessons that would be completed prior to the one-shot library session. But translating enthusiasm for those prerequisites to the rest of the instructors was not necessarily a given. There is no professional consequence for instructors who choose not to have students complete the prerequisites. In our experience with the first-year composition classes, the director of composition, who was on the Lesson Study team, promoted the prerequisites during professional development for first-year composition instructors and followed up at the appropriate time during the semester. She was able to speak to the ways that not complying with the prerequisite requirement undermines the students' experiences in class.

Even with a strong leadership role taken by allies in the department—in our case the director of composition—there is always the problem with optionality, not just with the prerequisites, but with all of the "extras" we develop. Even prerequisites for the one-shot that can be done outside of class are not always introduced before the one-shot session.

Cultivating faculty buy-in is something that takes effort and persistence. And even the faculty members reticent to try our "extras" recognize and appreciate our efforts. But sometimes it is not us, but faculty members themselves that are the best advocates for the "extra lessons." Word of mouth among instructors has led to exponential growth in the adoption of several of our lessons, as well as to the sharing of add-on projects and lesson modifications.

Consider Which Skills and Concepts Faculty Members Can Readily Teach

Here we refer to the relative difficulty of integrating some of these lessons into their already elaborated curriculum. How often do we hear faculty members say they have too much time and not enough content to cover in any given class? Never, in our experience. Most instructors are pressured by too much content and not enough class time to cover it. In our own experience working with writing faculty members, we could see that they were already taking on a new and densely scheduled curriculum. Especially because the new first-year composition curriculum included "Research and Inquiry" as one of its four goals, we wanted to do everything we could to decrease the chances that information literacy would be benched during the semester. It was integral to the course, yet still difficult to incorporate. It is for this reason that we sought to provide a mix of in-class and out-of-class learning opportunities, as well some short but content-rich videos. Some of our "extras" required no faculty intervention other than follow-through, and others had more extensive lesson plans that required active faculty participation.

Recognize and Mitigate Instructor Discomfort with Teaching Information Literacy

Even for faculty committed to incorporating the extra lessons, the thought of *teaching* them can be daunting. Teaching information literacy is not always easy for faculty. In his book *Teaching Research Processes: The Faculty Role in the Development of Skilled Student Researchers*, William Badke describes how many faculty, working in their own discipline, have developed specialized and idiosyncratic research patterns that are not easily replicated by their students.[5] By learning their subject area well, they have a familiarity with both what is available and how to access it. Some faculty find it useful to stay current with a specific set of journals or search primarily within their research specialty area. As a result, it is a challenge for faculty to reimagine their novice state: to return to the early days of their development as a researcher and understand the needs of their students. But for Badke, the goal is not to restrict information literacy instruction to librarians, but rather to give disciplinary faculty the tools to be able to recognize what their students need to learn about conducting research and how to deliver that in addition to the instruction provided by librarians.

Librarians can take several steps to mitigate the lack of confidence that some instructors have teaching information literacy and thereby facilitate the adoption of the supplemental materials and lessons.

- *Offer faculty training sessions.* It can be difficult to entice faculty to attend optional workshops and training sessions, but such sessions can be effective in building enthusiasm for and promoting adoption of library learning objects. Taking advantage of existing faculty meetings and training events is ideal if the opportunity presents itself. We have had success in getting ourselves added to departmental meetings by having a department chair or enthusiastic faculty-member ally add us to an agenda. In the case of our work with the first-year composition program, we were fortunate to be added to the agenda of the week-long professional development workshop that all instructors were required to attend prior to teaching in the program. Here we were able to introduce the one-shot lesson as well as the extras and demonstrate how they could be used. This gathering of instructors had the added benefit of endorsements from instructors who had successfully used some of the extras.
- *Supply documentation.* Develop sample lesson plans illustrating how the extras can be incorporated into a class or assigned as outside-of-class work. Offer suggested approaches for using the extras supplied by the library.
- *Demonstrate.* Even if limited library staff prevents librarians from routinely meeting multiple times with a class to teach the library session plus all the supplemental lessons, it may be possible for librarians to teach additional sessions when working with an instructor or a new lesson for the first time. This way the librarian can demonstrate how the extras can be used, and in subsequent classes, the instructor can assume the teaching of those supplementary lessons.
- *Work one-on-one with faculty.* Often, simply meeting with an instructor to discuss the inclusion of additional lessons is an effective method for preparing instructors to include a learning object for the first time.

Creating focused, flexible, and short learning objects, accompanied by ideas and examples for their use, increases the likelihood that instructors will incorporate them. As they are used by faculty in a variety of disciplines and courses, communicating with faculty about how they use them will provide librarians with additional examples and testimonials to promote their use.

NOTES

1. "Concept Maps," YouTube video, 3:48, posted by McIntyre Library, August 23, 2012, http://youtu.be/P2_BLScIWj0.

2. Shiao-Feng Su, "Design and Development of Web-Based Information Literacy Tutorials," *The Journal of Academic Librarianship* 36, no. 4 (2010): 320-28, doi:10.1016/j.acalib.2010.05.006; Meredith Farkas, "Tutorials That Matter: Learning Objects in the Library Instruction Program," *American Libraries* (July–August 2011): 32; Amy Gustavson, Angela Whitehurst, and David Hisle, "Laying the Information Literacy Foundation: A Multiple-Media Solution," *Library Hi Tech* 29, no. 4 (2011): 725–40; Lori S. Mestre, "Matching Up Learning Styles with Learning Objects: What's Effective?" *Journal of Library Administration* 50, no. 7/8 (2010): 808–29, doi:10.1080/01930826.2010.488975.

3. The Pennsylvania State University Libraries, "The Information Cycle: How Today's Events are Tomorrow's Information," Flash video, 2004, https://scholarsphere.psu.edu/files/8623j028r; "The Information Cycle," YouTube video, 6:56, posted by Kate Hinnant, September 17, 2012, http://youtu.be/FbaWMb7QDfQ.

4. James Herrick, *The History and Theory of Rhetoric: An Introduction* (Boston: Pearson, 2005), 11.

5. William Badke, *Teaching Research Processes: The Faculty Role in the Development of Skilled Student Researchers* (Whitney, UK: Chandos Publishing, 2012), 44.

7

The Benefits and
Challenges of Collaboration

In this chapter we will discuss the benefits and challenges of collaborating with faculty on designing an instruction session. Collaboration is something that librarians do inherently. For many, it begins in library school through the consistent use of group projects. Once we get into the profession, it is not uncommon for instruction librarians to collaborate with each other on developing a library instruction program or work on a specific class together. And although libraries have different departments (cataloging, reference, systems, acquisitions, collection development, etc.), these departments are not wholly independent from each other. It requires everyone in the library—such as catalogers who add descriptions to recently acquired items, systems librarians who maintain access to the library's electronic holdings, and instruction librarians who teach users how to access books and journal articles—for the library to serve its user base with the resources it needs. The library is by its nature a collaborative institution. Collaboration is required within the library to ensure that the organization functions effectively. And collaboration with external stakeholders is required to ensure that the library is meeting their needs.

Librarians are conditioned to collaborate, and our professional organizations acknowledge and advocate for this collaboration imperative. The Association of College & Research Libraries (ACRL) helps to direct instruction librarians with their "Guidelines for Instruction Programs in Academic Libraries." In it they suggest that "academic libraries work together with other members of their institutional communities to participate in, support, and achieve the educational mission of their institutions by teaching the core competencies of information literacy." Further, the guidelines encourage librarians to "seek opportunities for collaborative engagement in new institutional initiatives and redesigned curricula that allow for a deeper interplay between the library's instruction program and the total campus learning environment."[1] ACRL has another document that promotes collaboration between librarians and faculty. In their "Characteristics of Programs of Information Literacy that Illustrate Best Practices: A Guideline" document, one of the 10 characteristics that are considered best practices is collaboration. Furthermore, collaboration is explicitly stated as an important characteristic or is implied as important in all other categories through language such as "accommodat[ing] input from institutional stakeholders."[2] In short, it is essential that instruction librarians embrace collaboration.

Many librarians find that collaborating with faculty poses greater challenges than collaborating with their colleagues in the library. There are a number of reasons why this is the case.

- *Proximity*: Librarians generally work in proximity to other librarians. And this proximity goes beyond physical proximity of working in the same building; it also refers to structural and philosophical proximities that bring librarians together under unifying leadership, attending the same meetings and working toward shared goals. Teaching faculty, on the other hand, are usually in different buildings and in some cases on different campuses altogether. They attend their own departmental meetings, are physically located among their colleagues in their departments, and are focused on their own teaching and research responsibilities that at first glance do not place a high priority on collaboration with external departments.
- *Lack of assertiveness*: Librarians are arguably too reticent in their approach, yielding to faculty on content matters, even in information literacy, where librarians have a distinctive expertise. Librarians often must rely on teaching faculty as the conduit to students and, therefore, don't want to overstep and alienate faculty in inserting themselves into courses. Instead they defer to the faculty in what is included in a library instruction session, even when the request is unrealistic.
- *Faculty's competing interests*: Faculty schedules are filled with teaching, grading, advising, research, curricular development, and other departmental responsibilities. Additionally, most faculty lament lack of time to include all the content they would like to include in the allotted hours of a semester class. Adding one more thing to their list of responsibilities may tip the scale against collaborating with a librarian.
- *Different cultures*: We have discussed how librarians work in a culture of collaboration; this is not necessarily the case for most teaching faculty. They often work in a culture where autonomy reigns. Their schedules, research agendas, and areas of specialization allow and even encourage them to work independently. Collaboration is not usually on their radar the same way it is for librarians. Perceived faculty reluctance to collaborate has frustrated and even angered some librarians. One publication even went so far as to use language affiliated with war strategy to describe the relationship between that of the librarian and faculty member.

In the academic library, a successful strategy for infiltrating faculty lines and entrenching information literacy in the formal curriculum requires careful selection of personnel; rigorous intelligence gathering, to identify both allies and adversaries; and disciplined employment of both defensive and offensive tactics.[3]

Librarians would do well to respect that collaboration has not necessarily been a part of working culture of teaching faculty in the same way it has been for librarians, and to be mindful of different work cultures when proposing collaboration ideas to faculty.

Literature on faculty-librarian collaboration generally falls into one of two categories. The first category describes a specific collaborative project. Examples include Watson et al.'s description of collaboratively building an instruction session for a first-year composition class, Walter's description of course-integrated instruction in medieval studies, and Jacobson and Mackey's book that presents numerous case studies of collaborations between the library and various academic departments. While most collaborative projects center on a single course, some focus on an entire curriculum, such as Stombaugh et al.'s description of a scaffolded instruction program in the nursing curriculum.[4]

The other category of collaboration literature focuses on the state of the art of collaboration, describing recent studies. These literature reviews abound[5] and, not surprisingly, conclude that collaborating with faculty is a good thing. What is interesting to note when reviewing the literature is that the articles are overwhelmingly published in library-related journals, not in discipline-specific journals. Whether that is indicative of the relative importance placed on collaboration by faculty in other disciplines or whether it indicates less emphasis on the scholarship of teaching and learning in these disciplines, it remains the case that the vast majority of librarian-faculty collaboration research is written by and for librarians. From the numerous case studies and literature reviews there are several common findings or themes that emerge.

- Faculty see librarians as information literacy experts and thus turn to them for help teaching students library skills and information literacy concepts.[6] One faculty member went so far as to suggest that if he were to teach his students how to use the library that "would be like having a plumber try to teach students how to do heart surgery."[7]
- Librarians believe that a good working relationship with one faculty member will lead to other collaborations with different faculty members.[8]
- Librarians believe that if they have a good relationship with a faculty member, that faculty member will encourage students to use the library, resulting in an increase of usage among students.[9]
- Faculty report that collaborating with a librarian to provide library instruction results in better performance by their students.[10]
- Collaboration helps build a relationship of trust and respect between faculty and librarians.[11]
- By closely collaborating with faculty, librarians will be seen as academic equals on campus, which is a commonly stated goal.[12] As Zabel suggests, however, we

as librarians need to stop dwelling on our perception of the "lack of respect teaching faculty have for librarians." She says that "this negativism [by librarians] only marginalizes librarians and continues the perception that librarians are on the peripheral, taking a backseat to faculty when it comes to instructional issues."[13]

We will build on these themes, adding to the list of benefits, but also addressing the challenges of collaboration, an issue that receives less attention in the literature.

BENEFITS OF COLLABORATION

Planning Stage

Clearing up Misconceptions and Identifying Gaps

Part of the formation and planning stage of collaboration is the process of getting to know the members of the team, be it one other person or several. Just as with any relationship, as you get to know each other, you become aware of each other's strengths (and weaknesses). For example, some people are detail oriented, where others are big-picture thinkers, and in a collaboration environment you can begin to identify how those strengths can contribute to reaching the goals of the group. Recognize that discovering group dynamics and synergies is not wasted time but essential to productive collaboration. Again, not unlike any relationship, it can be helpful to know where a person has been. What history, experiences, and preconceived notions do they bring to the table? For the teaching faculty in the group, have they worked with librarians in the past on information literacy instruction? What went well? What fell short? What brings them to the table now? Librarians should share their experiences as well. What do they encounter when teaching in other classes? All parties will want to share their experiences and observations regarding what students need to know, what they appear to know, and what is assumed about what they know. By having these discussions early on, all team members can clear up any misconceptions that they may have of the other and come to a better understanding of what is known by students and what is reasonable to expect out of the collaboration. Through this process team members can identify gaps in the curriculum and identify where a collaboration might be beneficial.

Reducing Confusion

Through ongoing discussions, team members can explore areas of disagreement and distinguish differences of opinion from semantic differences. Sometimes differences are rooted in the inability to arrive at a shared language or way of describing the situation. For example, during our nursing Lesson Study planning stage, team members recognized early on that when nurses talk of evidence-based practice and librarians talk about information literacy, they are talking about many of the same concepts and ideas. Similarly, in our ongoing work with the first-year composition faculty, we continue to find commonalities between the rhetorical vocabulary used in the writing curriculum and our evolving definitions of information literacy. Finding common ground enables the team to move forward.

Becoming Equally Responsible

Library instruction is often couched in terms of providing a service to faculty and students, one that supports teaching and learning rather than one that is an integral part of teaching and learning in its own right. This is not to say that librarians should reject the idea that they provide a service. We *are* service oriented, and we should be proud of that. However, we also come to the table with our own brand of pedagogical experience and expertise regarding information literacy. Through collaboration with faculty, librarians can gain the confidence to assert their expertise rather than simply accommodating the wishes of the faculty and allowing them to drive the session. Instead of a one-way conversation in which the faculty tells the librarian what he/she expects of the librarian, the collaborative partnership leads to a give-and-take in which both parties plan a lesson on equal footing and take equal responsibility for its outcome.

Implementation Stage

Harmonizing Instruction

When librarians and faculty have a close collaboration in which both take responsibility for development of the lesson, the resulting lesson is much smoother. Both parties have an understanding of what the students will be doing the day of the instruction session so that when questions arise on lesson logistics, both the librarian and professor can answer. Similarly, if there are questions about the class assignment, which is likely the impetus for the lesson, the librarian will be familiar enough with it and with the professor's expectations to field some of those questions as well. When students see that their professor and the librarian have a shared understanding of what is happening during the lesson, it lends a certain gravitas to what is happening.

Creating a Support System

A collaborative relationship can be beneficial to the execution of the lesson when things go awry by providing a support system. Sometimes the best-laid plans don't work out. For instance, in one of our collaborations the professor got sick the day of the planned lesson. She had intended on using the first hour of a class to prepare the students for the library instruction session, which would occur during the second hour of class. The librarian and faculty had worked together closely so that the librarian was very familiar with the assignment and preparatory material that the professor had planned. Rather than scrapping the whole plan for the day, the librarian was able to step in and teach the content and assignment so that the library instruction session could still be taught.

Moving Forward

The end of a successful collaborative project doesn't mean that the collaboration has truly ended. The results of the collaboration can play out in several positive ways.

Sympathizing with Each Other

Both librarians and faculty will likely come away from the collaborative experience with a better understanding of the demands and priorities that the others face. Librarians, better able to understand how faculty work and what drives them, will be able to use that increased understanding to better communicate with faculty in the future. Likewise, faculty will have their perceptions of librarians changed and have a more complete awareness of the role that they play on campus.

Having an Advocate

Information literacy is often a loosely defined concept included in the list of outcomes we want for graduating college students. Faculty generally agree that it is a good thing but often assume that the students are developing these skills somewhere else, like in the library because librarians are typically the ones talking about

Figure 7.1.   Library and English faculty gathered for Lesson Study collaboration.
UWEC Photography

information literacy. As librarians know, however, information literacy is not a thing that is acquired in 50 minutes with a librarian, or even over the course of an entire semester. It's a skill that requires recursive practice, and thus it must be integrated into the entire curriculum. Librarians are often its champion, but to fully commit to the integration of information literacy, information literacy needs advocates beyond librarians. On our campus we have witnessed a burgeoning of support among faculty as a result of our collaborations. For example, the director of composition and her colleagues in the first-year composition program now take a more intentional and aggressive approach in integrating information literacy into the curriculum. She also states that she has a better understanding of the importance of information literacy and pays more attention to the literature on information literacy, including the development of the new ACRL *Framework* and its proposed threshold concepts. She is now a campus advocate for information literacy and discusses the concept with other faculty on campus. Faculty who have worked closely with librarians have a deeper appreciation of what librarians can do to assist faculty and students and are more likely, in our experience, to recommend librarians to their colleagues and to their students when a need arises.

Continuing Collaborations

One successful collaboration begets additional collaborative opportunities. As a result of our initial Lesson Study project with writing faculty on campus, librarians have been asked to become integrally involved in continuing curricular improvement efforts, professional development workshops for writing instructors, and ongoing assessment activity with composition faculty.

Increasing Visibility

Collaborations with faculty lead to an increased visibility of the library on campus and beyond. Faculty talk to each other; they also become aware of projects through other campus channels such as newsletters, various campus forums, and announcements of faculty publications and presentations. News of our Lesson Study project with the composition faculty caught the attention of other faculty on campus, and faculty in the sciences, social work, and nursing expressed interest in embarking on similar projects. Finally, with each successful collaboration, librarians are building their reputation as scholars of teaching and learning on campus.

CHALLENGES

As any student who has ever been assigned a group project can attest, collaboration is not without its challenges. Creating a lesson plan with faculty who are used to developing their curriculum individually, for example, can make collaboration especially difficult. Awareness of potential hurdles and possible strategies for dealing with a variety of challenges can keep these pitfalls from derailing the group's work.

Commitment Issues

Sometimes people express interest in participating in a group project, but they lack commitment to follow through. They may regularly miss meetings, be disengaged during meetings, or fail to complete assigned tasks. Solutions to this problem will depend largely on the organizational structure or structures within which the group operates. If there is a clear reporting structure, a supervisor can intervene to get the group member back on track or remove the individual from the group. If no such structure exists, as is likely with faculty from different disciplines, a group facilitator or team member—preferably one who is perceived as an official or unofficial leader—may be able to diplomatically approach the underperforming group member to discuss expectations and reassess the member's commitment to the project. If it is impractical or unadvisable to confront the member for political reasons, it may be best for the rest of the group to accept the fact of an underperforming member and simply move on.

Scheduling

Finding a time that everyone can meet can be difficult. In our experience we found it useful to schedule regular meetings for a semester at a time. That way, if the team needs to meet, it should already be on everyone's calendar. If a scheduled meeting is not needed, it can easily be canceled.

Differing Opinions

It is likely that differences of opinions will arise. We found that working with colleagues in different disciplines brings together not only a mix of personalities but also of working styles, pedagogical styles, and communication styles. Make sure everyone in the team has an opportunity to voice their opinion, but do not let one person stifle conversation or dominate discussion. This is where a skilled facilitator or team member is essential to bring the group together, encourage compromise or consensus, and move the group forward. When disagreements do arise, it is advisable to go back to the goals set by the team, reread them, and discuss how they affect the question at hand.

Obsessing over Details

It is likely that group members are invested in and passionate about the project, especially if their participation is more voluntary than compulsory. Sometimes the very passion that drives a project can hinder it when team members get bogged down in a particular issue and have difficulty letting it go or accepting the decision of the group. Again, a skilled facilitator can work to move the group forward, reiterating any ground rules set by the group or stating that the group operate at the will of the majority of members. Depending on the issue, it may be diplomatic and helpful to suggest a separate meeting designated to dealing solely with the issue, or to suggest that a disgruntled team member hold onto that thought and implement it in a separate, subsequent project.

Subgroups

While most collaborations will require that individuals or subgroups complete tasks outside of meeting times, generally it is not advisable for a self-designated subset of the team to develop a lesson plan outside of a group meeting. This activity may be viewed negatively by other team members who may see the individual or subgroup as attempting to commandeer the process. It may be awkward for other group members to critique the plan if it does not align with overall goals. And it may be more difficult to get group buy-in for a plan they felt they had no role in developing. While well-meaning group members may believe that developing a draft independently can save the group time, it could end up costing the group more time in negotiating and diplomatically undoing and redoing the work. It can also lead to hurt feelings when suggestions for the lesson's development aren't adopted by the group, thus inhibiting group dynamics. Should a group decide to assign a subgroup or individual to draft a lesson or significant portion of the lesson, strategies for critiquing that contribution should be clarified ahead of time so that there isn't an expectation that the draft be unilaterally accepted as presented.

Getting Buy-In from Other Colleagues

When a group collaborates on the development of a lesson plan, it may be the case that individuals outside of the group will be expected to adopt it. Such was the case with the lesson we developed for the first-year composition course. It was subsequently included in the standardized curriculum for the Blugold Seminar in Critical Reading and Writing. Most of the seminar instructors had not been a part of our Lesson Study team, so they didn't have the same investment in, enthusiasm for, or understanding of the established lesson. Let our initial mistake in scaling and unveiling our lesson to a larger audience help you to avoid the same. Basically, we included the lesson in the curriculum with insufficient information for instructors on how we envisioned integrating it with the rest of the curriculum and our thought processes in developing it. The first iterations of the lesson taught in classes where the seminar instructors had not participated in its development were met with a tepid response. As a result, we made some modifications to the lesson based on feedback, and then, working with the composition director, were more intentional in communicating the lesson's purpose, goals, and supplemental materials to instructors. Librarians were invited to participate in professional development workshops offered for new Blugold Seminar instructors. We used those workshops to introduce the librarians and the lesson, talk about its connection to the Blugold Seminar curriculum, and demonstrate the lesson. This approach resulted in much more positive feedback in following semesters. Similarly, librarians who hadn't been involved in developing the lesson were initially less enthusiastic about teaching it. We decided to extend the Lesson Study philosophy of peer observation to them and encouraged them to observe the lesson being taught by a team member before attempting to do so themselves. This allowed the observer to follow along with the lesson plan and see it implemented in a real-world environment. It's one thing to have a lesson described to you or to read a lesson plan; it is an entirely different thing to see it in action. After having your colleagues observe the lesson, meet to go over any questions they may have. Ask them what they think worked well, what didn't, or if they have any suggestions for improvement. Modeling the continuous revision of Lesson Study offers an avenue for bringing colleagues into the fold, making them more invested in the lesson that they now have a voice in improving.

Longitudinal Challenges

Longer multiyear projects raise the likelihood that members of the group may change before the project is complete. Changes in the group, regardless of the reasons, can pose difficulties in maintaining the integrity of the goals that the group established.

Extended Absences

In the course of our multiyear collaboration with nursing faculty, three of the seven members of the team went on parental leave. We learned that having a group member rejoin a group after an extended leave requires some planning and effort. While it is always a good idea to take notes or minutes at meetings to summarize discussion and decisions made, it is especially important to do so when a member is absent. Based on our experience, we recommend that the group hold a reintegration meeting when the team member rejoins it after the extended absence. At the meeting, the returning member can be brought up to speed on progress made in his or her absence. Team members should review next steps in the process and go over the goals again to make sure that the scope of the project is understood. It is important to set aside time for a reintegration meeting because group dynamics will likely have changed during the absence. Returning members should recognize that it is rarely advisable to attempt to change the direction taken or decisions made by the rest of the group during their absence.

Losing a Team Member

It is not uncommon in projects of long duration to lose a team member. People leave their positions, get reassigned to different projects, become overcommitted and have to give up something, or otherwise find it necessary to discontinue participation in a group. The team will have to decide whether or not it makes sense to replace the team member. Can remaining team members assume the responsibilities of the departing member? Does the departing team member have an essential skill set, expertise, or perspective that will be lost if not replaced by another member? Is there someone available who has the necessary expertise, time, and interest to join the group? Depending on where you are in the process of your multiyear project, you may find that adding a new team member is not feasible. The team should carefully consider group dynamics and how far along the team is.

Adding a New Team Member

A group may decide to add a new member, to replace a departing member, or to add a necessary and unrepresented perspective or expertise. Sometimes adding a new member can help a group that has stalled or isn't functioning optimally. A new person can bring fresh ideas and a different perspective and a necessary change to group dynamics. Be aware that when a new member is added for any reason, group dynamics will shift. The group should expect a period of again working through— albeit perhaps in abbreviated style—the four stages of team development (forming, storming, norming, and performing) that Tuckman describes.[14] Efforts must be made to ensure that the new member feels like a part of the group rather than an outsider. One strategy is to have the facilitator or person acting as team leader sit down with the new team member and describe the project, its history, goals, and where they are in the process. Ample time should be given for questions. The team facilitator or leader should also talk to the team members about adding a new member, why it is important, and what they can do to help integrate this person into the multiyear project.

THE END OF THE COLLABORATION . . . OR IS IT?

Maintaining the momentum of a collaboration and continuous revision can be difficult once the completion of the original project has been reached. After so much time, effort, and thought have been put into a single lesson, it is tempting to consider it complete, definitive, and unchangeable. In reality, it is none of those. Something will inevitably change—library search tools, course content, pedagogical standards, even your own evolving thoughts—that will require continued revision and collaboration. If your collaboration was a success, the rapport that was developed will make it much easier for the group to communicate what needs to be changed. When revising after the end of a formal collaboration, always keep the lesson's goals in mind. It is even possible that the context in which and for which you developed the lesson has shifted, and the goals themselves need to be reconsidered.

Finally, keep in mind that even success itself can be a challenge. As mentioned earlier, one successful collaboration can lead to others. What if the collaboration was so successful that it generates interest from other faculty beyond which you can reasonably manage? Consider enlisting colleagues who weren't involved in previous projects to become involved. Our library has taken on a Lesson Study culture of sorts in that interest and involvement in Lesson Study projects is steadily spreading throughout our ranks. If you are lucky enough to have demand that exceeds your resources, prioritize. Choose collaborations that are well timed with other curricular developments or that offer the greatest benefit for the most students or for the institution. If library staff are currently maxed out, set a time in the future for beginning a collaboration and keep lines of communication open until then. Managing demand, while challenging, is a good problem to have.

NOTES

1. "Guidelines for Instruction Programs in Academic Libraries," Association of College & Research Libraries, last revised October 2011, http://www.ala.org/acrl/standards/guidelines instruction.

2. "Characteristics of Programs of Information Literacy that Illustrate Best Practices: A Guideline," Association of College & Research Libraries, last revised January 2012, http://www.ala.org/acrl/standards/characteristics.

3. Katherine Beaty Chiste, Andrea Glover, and Glenna Westwood, "Infiltration and Entrenchment: Capturing and Securing Information Literacy Territory in Academe," *Journal of Academic Librarianship* 26, no. 3 (2000): 202.

4. Shevaun E. Watson et al., "Revising the 'One-Shot' through Lesson Study: Collaborating with Writing Faculty to Rebuild a Library Instruction Session," *College & Research Libraries* 74, no. 4 (2013): 381–98, doi:10.5860/crl12-255; Scott Walter, "Engelond: A Model for Faculty-Librarian Collaboration in the Information Age," *Information Technology and Libraries* 19, no. 1 (2000): 34–41; Trudi E. Jacobson and Thomas P. Mackey, eds., *Information Literacy Collaborations that Work* (New York: Neal-Schuman Publishers, Inc., 2007); Angie Stombaugh et al., "Using Lesson Study to Integrate Information Literacy throughout the Curriculum," *Nurse Educator* 38, no. 4 (2013): 173–77, doi:10.1097/NNE.0b013e318296db56.

5. Maryam Derakhshan and Diljit Singh, "Integration of Information Literacy into the Curriculum: A Meta-Synthesis," *Library Review* 60, no. 3 (2011): 218–29; Wade R. Kotter, "Bridging the Great Divide: Improving Relations Between Librarians and Classroom Faculty," *The Journal of Academic Librarianship* 25, no. 4 (1999): 294–303; Michael Mounce, "Working Together: Academic Librarians and Faculty Collaborating to Improve Students' Information Literacy Skills: A Literature Review 2000–2009," *The Reference Librarian* 51, no. 4 (2010): 300–20, doi:10.1080/02763877.2010.501420.

6. Donald H. Dilmore, "Librarian/Faculty Interaction at Nine New England Colleges," *College & Research Libraries* 57, no. 3 (1996): 274–84; Kate Manuel, Susan E. Beck, and Molly Molloy, "An Ethnographic Study of Attitudes Influencing Faculty Collaboration in Library Instruction," *The Reference Librarian* 43, no. 89/90 (2005): 139–61, doi:10.1300/J120v43n89_10.

7. Manuel et al., "An Ethnographic Study," 147–48.

8. Kotter, 294.

9. L. Sanborn, "Improving Library Instruction: Faculty Collaboration," *Journal of Academic Librarianship* 31, no. 5 (2005): 477–81, doi: 10.1016/j.acalib.2005.05.010; Anne G. Lipow, "Outreach to Faculty: Why and How," in *Working with Faculty in the New Electronic Library*, ed. Linda Shirato (Ann Arbor, MI: Pierian Press, 1992), 7–13; Robert K. Baker, "Working with Our Teaching Faculty," *College & Research Libraries* 56, no. 5 (1995): 377–79.

10. Shun Han Rebekah Wong and Dianne Cmor, "Measuring Association between Library Instruction and Graduation GPA," *College & Research Libraries* 72, no. 5 (2011): 464–73, doi:10.5860/crl-151; Susan Hurs and Joseph Leonard, "Garbage In, Garbage Out: The Effect of Library Instruction on the Quality of Students' Term Papers," *Electronic Journal of Academic and Special Librarianship* 8, no. 1 (2007), accessed January 3, 2015, http://southernlibrarianship.icaap.org/content/v08n01/hurst_s01.htm; Manuel et al., "An Ethnographic Study," 154.

11. Ruth Ivey, "Information Literacy: How Do Librarians and Academics Work in Partnership to Deliver Effective Learning Programs?" *Australian Academic & Research Libraries* 34, no. 2 (2003): 100–13, doi:10.1080/00048623.2003.10755225; Dick Raspa and Dane Ward, "Listening for Collaboration: Faculty and Librarians Working Together," in *The Collaborative Imperative*, ed. Dick Raspa and Dane Ward (Chicago: American Library Association, 2000), 1–18.

12. Robert T. Ivey, "Teaching Faculty Perceptions of Academic Librarians at Memphis State University," *College & Research Libraries* 55, no. 1 (1994): 69–82.

13. Diane Zabel, "A Reaction to 'Information Literacy and Higher Education,'" *The Journal of Academic Librarianship* 30, no. 1 (2004): 18.

14. Bruce W. Tuckman, "Developmental Sequence in Small Groups," *Psychological Bulletin* 63, no. 6 (1963): 384–99.

8

Organizational Considerations

It has become clear by now that rethinking and reinvigorating the one-shot library instruction model requires a great deal of effort on the part of librarians. A librarian may consider the time that such planning, collaborating, assessing, and revising will require and question if such an undertaking is feasible. Rare is the library that can add positions or resources for such projects, and our own library was no exception. With a recent wave of retirements and budget cuts, our total number of librarians had decreased in the preceding decade. Like so many libraries, we were struggling to do more with less. At the same time, the library was experiencing a change in use patterns. These conditions, in no way unique to our library, provided an ideal incentive for and climate within which to reassess priorities and responsibilities of librarians and library support staff. Rather than adding to what we were already doing, we needed to make decisions about changing what we were doing. While the direct work of revising the one-shot fell primarily to the instruction librarians, redistributing responsibilities and priorities was a library-wide affair.

The first thing we looked at was how instruction librarians spend their time. For decades, libraries have been debating the efficacy of having librarians staff the reference desk. The pre-Internet reference desk fielded a high frequency of ready-reference and in-depth questions requiring intimate knowledge of reference and library resources; post-Internet has brought about a change in reference desk activity, with an increase in technology questions, a decrease in ready-reference quick and discrete-answer questions, and the opportunity for librarians to engage in more in-depth research consultations with students. In this environment, is it cost-effective to have professional librarians sitting at a reference desk, awaiting meaty research questions while fixing stapler and printer jams? In our library, librarians were reluctant to give up their time at the reference desk. They enjoyed it, quite frankly, and believed that the randomness of their interactions there kept them grounded in and aware of user needs. However, they were also aware that less time spent staffing the desk would mean more time available to focus on their teaching and liaison roles. As a compromise, librarian time at the desk was reduced from about 10 to 15 hours a week staffing the reference desk to about 4 or 5. Librarians were also relieved of weekend and evening hours.

In order to make this change, the library had to act holistically. Still committed to keeping the reference desk staffed, the library turned to paraprofessional staff. But paraprofessional staff had to come from somewhere. A shift from print to electronic collections coupled with shared cataloging and reduced collections budgets overall meant that demand for cataloging staff was declining. Staff was reallocated from technical to public services as a result. Such changes do not typically occur without some resistance, but a clearly articulated vision from library administration helps ease transitions. In our case, we took advantage of attrition to ease in the changes. As has been noted in the literature, when paraprofessionals assume responsibilities once handled by professionals, usually at a lower rate of pay than librarians, there can be some understandable resentment.[1] Over a period of several years, our library worked to reclassify these evolving paraprofessional positions to recognize, in terms of title and compensation, the increased responsibility.

Relieved of some previous responsibilities, how were librarians to move in the new direction of focusing on teaching and collaboration with faculty? After all, one does not simply engage in collaborative efforts with faculty without initiating and establishing a level of trust, camaraderie, and shared goals.

Efforts to develop meaningful collaborations with faculty can be grouped into three interrelated categories: networking, knowing the faculty, and becoming directly involved in the life of the institution.

NETWORKING

More comfortable for some librarians than others, networking with faculty, staff, administrators, and students is imperative to ensuring that the library and librarians are serving a vital role on campus. For the librarian accustomed to staffing a reference desk—waiting, ready, and willing to respond to questions when they come—making an effort to leave one's comfortable turf to meet and converse with others can be disconcerting. It can even feel frivolous. The first thing to remember is that networking is working. Conversations over coffee and small talk at retirement parties are often where collaborations ignite. Librarians must embrace the idea that attending events that put them in touch with colleagues in other departments is now part of their job. By making an effort to put themselves in places where they are likely to meet others, the librarians are setting the stage for collaboration. Small talk can lead to bigger talk, either immediately or as familiarity sets in and relationships and ideas begin to take shape. In a casual survey of librarian colleagues at our institution, we learned that professional relationships grew out of such varied events as the following:

- Attending new faculty orientation
- Dropping children off at the campus daycare
- Using campus recreation facilities such as the swimming pool or the gym
- Participating in campus wellness activities such as group yoga or intramural sports teams
- Joining book groups, both professional and recreational
- Attending receptions, celebrations, and other events on campus
- Joining community groups and volunteer organizations
- Attending neighborhood parties and get-togethers
- Participating in campus committees

Librarians have even created events to put themselves in contact and develop good will with others on campus who may not frequent the library. These are some examples:

- At the end of fall semester, librarians (some donning reindeer antlers or Santa hats) have walked through campus buildings distributing candy canes with uplifting or humorous messages attached. This provided an opportunity to introduce themselves to faculty, answer questions about library services, remind colleagues about the library, and begin to build familiarity that can lead to meaningful collaborations down the road.
- Librarians hosted a weekly viewing and discussion series of TED Talks that appealed to and drew a diverse swath of participants. Not focused on "library" issues per se, this series was able to put librarians in contact with other faculty where some discussion would inevitably lead to library-related topics.
- Librarians planned and offered a series of workshops on scholarly communication during Open Access Week, including practical and essential information such as negotiating publishing contracts and considering open-access journals.

Note that these networking opportunities do not take place only on campus; they include social events and connections developed where librarians work, live, and play, so to speak. To make the most of these opportunities, librarians are encouraged to move outside of what is for many their comfort zone: other librarians. When attending events, librarians should avoid the temptation to sit with immediate colleagues; rather, they are encouraged to approach someone they do not know well, someone they know from another context, or someone they know something about. This leads us to the next category of networking.

KNOWING THE FACULTY

Knowing something about the faculty, such as their research or teaching interests, their outside interests, their children, or their background, doesn't have to be as creepy as it sounds. It is simply a way of establishing a connection. That connection can be a shared professional interest, an outside interest, or just enough demonstrated interest in another person to initiate a conversation. Knowing something about faculty colleagues prepares librarians to be able to engage in conversation when they find themselves in networking situations. It also gives them a hook to use in initiating a networking situation. This sample list of ideas for learning about faculty colleagues is not exhaustive. Nor is it recommended that a librarian employ them all. That *would* be creepy!

- Read campus communications such as faculty and departmental newsletters, alumni news, and campus news releases.
- Attend faculty presentations of research and/or pedagogy on campus. For faculty in different disciplines this may manifest itself in different ways. For example in the visual and performing arts, this might include recitals, concerts, art openings, or theater productions.
- Attend faculty/student research fairs.
- Keep up with faculty publications and research achievements. This information may be conveyed in aforementioned campus publications. You can also set up RSS feeds in many databases so that you are notified of publications by faculty from your institution. (For more information, please see http://libguides.uwec .edu/uwecfeeds.)
- Follow faculty colleagues on social media. Use discretion here, and be sensitive to local cultural queues. On our campus, we have found that many faculty engage in professional and intellectual conversations via social media, and in some professional circles it has been an effective way to learn about others' interests and to engage.

The idea of getting to know and keeping up with all of the faculty on a campus, regardless of the size of the institution, is likely untenable. Many academic libraries, ours included, have moved to a "liaison" model, which pairs librarians with specific disciplines, departments, units, and colleges on campus. When we shifted from the "generalist" model, where librarians spent more time at the reference desk and taught for any and all departments upon request, to a liaison model, where librarians were assigned to specific departments, opportunities for communication and collaboration flourished. Our reorganization enabled us to introduce, or reintroduce, ourselves to faculty as "their" librarian. Some hadn't really given much thought to the library in the past, and the announcement that they now had a designated librarian captured their attention. They had a sense of the library providing them with a service they hadn't had before. Though the services all existed in the past, the new targeted approach made them feel new. Librarians offered services such as one-on-one consultations with faculty and students, teaching of library sessions, collaboration on developing research assignments, embedded librarians in online classes, and more. We saw an increase in referrals of students to liaison librarians. We experienced an increase in faculty contacting their liaison librarian with their own research questions. Some departments invited liaison librarians to departmental meetings, receptions, and graduation events. The liaison model allowed librarians to focus on the activities of their assigned departments and faculty, making the efforts in *knowing the faculty* more manageable. Of course, not all departments or faculty responded to the liaison model. Some still had very little interaction with the library. But that was OK. Librarians would have been unable to handle demand had all faculty immediately taken advantage of the offerings. What we have found is that the liaison model gradually grows in popularity over a span of several years. Word of mouth within departments results in steady growth of the program. Faculty turnover grows the program as new faculty are often more receptive to services than senior faculty who have their established ways of doing things. The liaison model has enabled us to establish the relationships that form the basis for more extensive and sustained collaboration such as the Lesson Study projects.

BECOMING DIRECTLY INVOLVED IN THE LIFE OF THE INSTITUTION

Closely related to knowing the faculty is knowing and being actively engaged in the campus. Librarians have long struggled with misperceptions by faculty of what librarians do, often viewing them in subordinate service roles rather than as teachers in their own right.[2] Further, faculty are less interested than librarians in addressing any disconnections or initiating collaborations. It is therefore up to librarians to raise awareness of what they do, demonstrate their importance to the mission of the institution, and actively position themselves as educators. Doing so requires that librarians understand and internalize the mission of the institution; become actively involved in committees, decisions, and profession development at the campus level; and assert themselves as teachers. Librarians must get out of the library. They must develop a holistic view of the institution and continually assess and reassess their role in it and the contributions they can make to it. How they do this will depend on the culture of the institution, what their status enables them to do, and their sheer level of moxie. The following are some suggested strategies.

Become Involved in Shared Governance on Campus

This is where many campus discussions take place, where priorities are articulated, and where various constituencies air their concerns and issues. Librarians are fortunate in that they often know faculty and staff across campus. There is also a sense that the library is "neutral territory," whereas departments, disciplines, and colleges often see themselves in competition with each other for limited resources. Exposure from working across disciplines combined with their perceived agnosticism can favor librarians in shared governance elections.

Join Committees, Especially Those Relating to Curriculum, Teaching, and Research

Through their participation, librarians learn the language, can better frame library initiatives using the shared language, and raise their profile on campus as committed educators. As part of its *Analyzing Your Instructional Environment* workbook, the Association of College & Research Libraries (ACRL) provides a "Campus Environmental Scanning" worksheet[3] that aids in identifying the campus groups whose activities librarians should be participating in or monitoring. On our campus, librarians hold positions on the campus-wide committees for assessment, academic policies, and university liberal education. These committees drive the curricular discussions and decisions of our campus, and were the driving forces behind major liberal education reform. The librarian voices on these committees ensured that the concept of information literacy made it into the liberal education learning outcomes. Now that these outcomes have been adopted, they provide added incentive for faculty to partner with librarians in ensuring their courses adequately address information literacy. But in addition to acting as advocates for information literacy, librarian involvement in curricular planning and assessment has gotten librarians out of the library and put them at the table with other faculty, raising their profile as educators on campus.

Engage in Curriculum Mapping

Collaborate with faculty in a process of identifying what is taught, when, and how, throughout a sequence of courses. Through this process, librarians and faculty can plot where progressive information literacy one-shot sessions can be integrated. The process of examining and discussing the curriculum and shared outcome goals inevitably leads to increased collaboration and collegiality.[4]

Shared Programming

Cosponsor local conferences, research-based events, literary and academic speakers, student affairs programming, and so on, with other departments and units.

Teach Credit Courses

If the institution allows it, librarians should look for opportunities to teach courses for credit. If the library doesn't offer credit courses, it may be possible for librarians to teach in other departments or programs, such as honors, general education, or an appropriate discipline. For librarians, the opportunity can shed light on the challenges and issues that teaching faculty face and create a shared experience on which future communication and collaboration can build.

Partner with Student Academic-Support Offices

On most college campuses, impressive and innovative things are being done in offices that support teaching and learning. Meeting and collaborating with offices such as a writing center, college transition programs, McNair Scholars Program, residence life, orientation, career services, and so on, can offer untold opportunity and inspiration.

Use the Reference Desk to Your Advantage

Although working fewer hours at the reference desk reduces the likelihood of librarians seeing patterns in questions asked by students, there are still opportunities to take advantage of common questions. If a librarian notices a pattern in questions being asked by students of a particular class, the librarian can talk directly with the faculty member and suggest that library instruction may be useful for the class. Sometimes this suggestion is more effective coming from the students themselves. When working with students from a class that could benefit from library instruction, the librarian can suggest to them that if they found the intervention useful, they should mention it to their professor as something from which the entire class could benefit.

Incentivizing Collaboration

As every librarian knows, not all faculty are eager to work together on incorporating one-shot library instruction into their curriculum. Sometimes, it may be necessary to incentivize. In our case, the Center for Excellence in Teaching and Learning (CETL) was able to offer stipends to faculty who worked on Lesson Study projects. However, a library could also apply for grant funding to compensate faculty for working with librarians during summer (noncontract) months to integrate or improve information literacy components of their courses. Some library budgets may be flexible enough to allocate a small stipend each year for this activity. If not a stipend, other less costly incentives can be effective in some situations. Many faculty, like students, respond favorably to free food, so hosting a luncheon in the library for new faculty, a midsemester coffee break, or an end-of-semester wine and cheese reception affords librarians the opportunity to talk to faculty about their research interests and also pitch the idea of the one-shot.

The thing to keep in mind about many of these activities is that while they may feel like a departure from traditional library work, they are essential if librarians are to do what they have always done, that is, adapt to changing demands, expectations, and needs. Librarians no longer need to focus instruction on how to use the tools of research. Instead, they are focusing on higher order skills to make sense of the content. This level of instruction demands much closer alignment with course content, so librarians need to know what is going on across campus. Understanding and being involved in curricular issues is the new work of instruction librarians. As the landscape changes in libraries, on college campuses, and in society in general, libraries must continue to identify areas of need and how to address them. They need to be on the lookout for the "white space" and nimble enough to fill it. They no longer have the luxury of assuming that they are universally regarded as the heart of the campus, but rather they must continually adapt to ensure they remain relevant and provide value. A key to demonstrating and improving value is assessment.

ASSESSMENT

Librarians, like other educators, sometimes harbor a love/hate relationship with assessment. In the worst cases it can feel like a bean-counting mandate from external forces, disconnected from the mission, focused on the wrong things: a distraction from "real" work. However, meaningful assessment can provide compelling and motivating information that helps librarians communicate and build on the value of the library. Megan Oakleaf, a leader in library assessment, writes, "While libraries have a long history of offering instructional resources and services . . . they have less experience assessing their impact in ways that have campuswide relevance. In order to avoid library-centric conceptions of instruction, librarians need to view instruction from a campuswide standpoint."[5] Not only do librarians need to understand and actively engage in the life of the institution, they need to assess their impact in terms shared by the institution. In the case of Lesson Study projects, this can mean aligning library outcome goals with those of the partnering department and/or the institution. The goals may be defined internally, such as through course or program goals, or they may be defined at a broader level. Our institution is guided by newly adopted liberal education learning goals, based loosely on some of the Association of American Colleges & Universities (AAC&U) Liberal Education and America's Promise (LEAP) Value rubrics.[6] Additionally, institutions are guided by accrediting bodies and increasingly by governmental accountability measures. We found that the Lesson Study process established the necessary relationships to move assessment of library instruction from an internal, library-centric level to a more holistic institutional level. Through the Lesson Study collaborations, librarians gained access to student data and performance artifacts previously unavailable to them.

In our library, like others, we have experimented with various assessment models. Most have been somewhat limited in scope due to lack of time and access to students. They have included brief pretests and posttests, evaluation forms filled out at the end of class by students, and online feedback forms e-mailed to students and faculty after instruction sessions. The student evaluations are moderately enlightening, generally polite, and positive, and usually provide feedback on the librarian's in-class "performance" more than reflective comments about content. Faculty feedback tends to be more constructive, as we usually solicit it after research papers have been turned in and graded. That way faculty can comment on their perception of the impact of library instruction on their students' research.

Oakleaf goes on to say that "by assessing students, librarians determine what students know and are able to do and, as a part of that process, librarians learn to be better teachers."[7] Framing assessment in terms of not only what the students learn but what the teacher learns to improve practice is at the heart of Lesson Study. Oakleaf and others refer to it as "reflective practice." Traditional feedback has enabled us to tweak our teaching, but the Lesson Study collaborations allowed us to take our assessment, and reflective practice, to a higher level. Even without looking at student performance outcomes, the Lesson Study process provides insights into student behaviors during a lesson, as observed by frank and impartial peers. This information is enough to start librarians on the road to reflective practice, working with colleagues to revisit and revise the way they teach.

Lesson Study is by definition assessment. It involves a group of individuals, a community of practice, working together to design and implement a lesson, observe it as it unfolds, reflect on what happened, revise, and do it again. Additional assessment measures can be built into the Lesson Study model, supplementing those inherent in the process. In our initial Lesson Study with the first-year composition program, we sought feedback from the students immediately following the lesson in the form of focus groups. We also had them fill out evaluation forms. And we collected the brief worksheets they filled out as part of the lesson to assess their selection of sources and their ability to adequately document the source so that it could be found again. In most cases, the student feedback confirmed and elaborated on what we were able to observe: They wanted more time for searching. They were not interested in documenting sources on a paper worksheet but instead were more likely to e-mail their search results to themselves or to their research partner as appropriate. This was obvious to us—after we observed it—and we changed the lesson accordingly. The multimodal approaches to assessment for this class were only possible because the instructor of the course, a member of the Lesson Study team, was willing to devote additional class time to completing them. This level of access to students had previously been unavailable to librarians.

Different Lesson Study collaborations lend themselves to different forms of supplemental assessment. The Lesson Study team working with the nursing curriculum saw the potential to incorporate a longitudinal study of students' information literacy skills. They also designed the study so that there would be a control group and they could compare data on students who engaged in the Lesson Study sequence of interventions with that of students who were not in the study cohort. The Nursing Lesson Study included the following assessments:

- *Peer observation of the lesson, as an inherent part of Lesson Study*: In the nursing project, the team was able to invite colleagues from the previous Lesson Study who were not a part of this one to serve as additional observers. Because these colleagues were familiar with the method of observation employed in Lesson

Study but not familiar with or invested in the lesson itself, they were able to
provide relatively unbiased feedback.

- *Pretest/posttests*: Students in the cohort took a pretest prior to the initial library
intervention during their sophomore year and a posttest when they were ready
to graduate after three years of library interventions. Students in a control group
took the same posttest prior to graduation. They received no interventions and
did not take the pretest.

- *In-class worksheets*: In each of the three library one-shot sessions that comprised
this study, students completed in-class worksheets. These were collected and
assessed by librarians and nursing faculty.

- *Embedded questions in midterm and final exams*: Questions related to the library
instruction were embedded into course midterm and final exams during the
three-year study to assess student comprehension. Control-group student exams
did not include these questions.

- *Focus groups*: Similar to the first-year composition Lesson Study, this lesson
study was able to carve out time for soliciting student feedback through focus
groups thanks to the nursing faculty member's willingness to devote class time
to this endeavor.

Initial collaborations like Lesson Study can open the door to more robust and sustained collaborations. Such has been the case with the first-year composition Lesson
Study. Following the initial Lesson Study, the English department undertook a major
revision of the freshman composition program from which arose the ambitious Blugold Seminar in Critical Reading and Writing. Its emphasis on critical thinking and
rhetorical analysis meshed with the tenets of information literacy. The partnership
between the English Department and the library formed via Lesson Study continued with the implementation of the new Blugold Seminar. So, too, did assessment.
The curricular revision included extensive assessment of student writing, and so the
infrastructure was there to focus on student research and inquiry, one of the four
goal areas of the Blugold Seminar. Prompted by a call for proposals to participate in
a program called Assessment in Action (AiA), sponsored by the Association of College & Research Libraries, the library submitted an assessment proposal to look at
information literacy outcomes of students in the Blugold Seminar. UW–Eau Claire
was accepted as one of 75 libraries from around the United States to participate in a
14-month program to develop a project that assesses the library's impact on student
learning.

We chose this project for the AiA grant because the Blugold Seminar is now a
common learning experience among all UW–Eau Claire students. This means that
our information literacy instruction lesson will reach up to 2,000 students annually.
A team comprising a librarian, the director of composition, and the campus director
of assessment was formed to design the assessment. They developed a rubric for assessing three outcomes that combined information literacy and rhetorical concepts.
Still underway as of this writing, the project brings composition instructors and

librarians together to read and assess student writing projects based on that rubric. A team of three librarians and three Blugold Seminar instructors met to review and discuss the rubric, which assessed three skills:

- Attribution of sources
- Evaluation of sources
- Communication of evidence

Through a norming process, the participants shared their interpretations of evidence of these skills and practiced assessing student writing using the rubric to ensure consistency in scoring. Though the project is not yet complete, even early into this project, the assessment is having an impact on the integration of information literacy instruction into the Blugold Seminar. The discussions that took place during norming sessions further enhanced librarian understanding of composition faculty goals, and vice versa. Librarians enjoyed the opportunity to review student writing that resulted in part from the library session. While at times it was discouraging to read substandard attempts at incorporating research into a paper, this opportunity was enlightening for librarians who rarely get a chance to see, much less assess, student outcomes at this level. Already discussions are ensuing between librarians and composition faculty to revise the information literacy components of the Blugold Seminar based on preliminary results.

In conclusion, there are many organizational considerations that can lead to an increased level of library one-shot instruction. Assessment, a move toward library liaisons, increased networking within the institution, getting to know faculty more personally, and becoming more directly involved in the life of the institution are all ways that seemingly small collaborative efforts can blossom into continually improving relationships. Through the collaborative process, as shared goals are articulated and increased levels of trust are attained, librarians are afforded a new status as partners in the teaching and learning process.

NOTES

1. Gillian S. Gremmels, "Staffing Trends in College and University Libraries," *Reference Services Review* 41, no. 2 (2013): 235, doi:10.1108/00907321311326165.

2. Lars Christianson, Mindy Stombler, and Lyn Thaxton, "A Report on Librarian-Faculty Relations from a Sociological Perspective," *Journal of Academic Librarianship* 30, no. 2 (2004): 119, doi:10.1016/j.acalib.2004.01.003; Kristin Anthony, "Reconnecting the Disconnects: Library Outreach to Faculty as Addressed in the Literature," *College & Undergraduate Libraries* 17, no. 1 (2010): 80, doi:10.1080/10691310903584817; Robert T. Ivey, "Reaching Faculty Perceptions of Academic Librarians at Memphis State University," *College & Research Libraries* 55, no. 1 (1994): 79.

3. Association of College & Research Libraries, "Analyzing Your Instructional Environment: A Workbook" (working paper, Association of College & Research Libraries Instruction

Section, 2010), 59, accessed January 4, 2015, http://www.ala.org/acrl/files/aboutacrl/directory ofleadership/sections/is/iswebsite/projpubs/aie/aie.pdf.

4. Mary Moser et al., "A More Perfect Union: Campus Collaborations for Curriculum Mapping Information Literacy Outcomes," in *A Declaration of Interdependence: Proceedings of the Fifteenth National Conference of the Association of College and Research Libraries, March 30–April 2, 2011, Philadelphia, PA*, ed. Dawn M. Mueller (Chicago: Association of College & Research Libraries, 2011), 330–39; Kay Pippin Uchiyama and Jean L. Radin, "Curriculum Mapping in Higher Education: A Vehicle for Collaboration," *Innovative Higher Education* 33, no. 4 (2009): 271–80, doi:10.1007/s10755-008-9078-8.

5. Megan Oakleaf, "Are They Learning? Are We? Learning Outcomes and the Academic Library," *Library Quarterly* 81, no. 1 (2011): 67, doi:10.1086/657444.

6. Terrel L. Rhodes, ed., *Assessing Outcomes and Improving Achievement: Tips and Tools for Using Rubrics* (Washington, DC: Association of American Colleges & Universities, 2010).

7. Oakleaf, 70.

9

Fine-Tuning the One-Shot

We have discussed strategies for rethinking the one-shot lesson, for cultivating relationships with instructors, for building upon the one-shot, and for planning, conducting, and assessing the one-shot lesson. Even with the supportive structure built around the library instruction session, a residual fear may still linger: this is our one shot and we don't want to blow it. This chapter looks at things that can pose challenges and offers strategies for preventing problematic situations and troubleshooting those things that inevitably go wrong.

BUILDING RAPPORT IN MINUTES

In the one-shot session, librarians have a lot of ground to cover. On top of that, they have the added challenge of trying to develop rapport and trust with a group of students almost immediately. Librarians share this challenge with public speakers, sales people, and comedians, whose success also relies on their ability to establish a connection with a group of people in a limited amount of time, often just minutes. Advice for public speakers on building rapport with an audience works for librarians, too. According to *Brilliant Public Speaking*, rapport can be established in just a couple of minutes by showing that you care, demonstrating that you understand your audience's (or students') issues, and indicating how you are going to help.[1] A simple statement can begin to address all three points; for example, "I understand that you have an exploratory essay to write. Some of you may have a pretty good idea of what you want to write about. Others of you may still be tossing around some general ideas. Don't worry, we will learn how to find the resources that will best help you no matter where you are in the process."

But let's back up a bit. Librarians often have a few valuable minutes before the instruction session commences that they can use strategically. Before class, as students arrive, is an important time for the librarian to begin gathering data about the group that she can then use to build rapport. As the students come in, do they seem to know each other? Are they talking to each other? Or do they instead sit down and look at their phones or computers, or quietly face the front of the classroom waiting for something to happen? Zoller and Landry talk about two kinds of groups: those with *high internal familiarity*, where individuals already know each other, and those with *low internal familiarity*, where they do not know each other.[2] The librarian can observe student behavior to assess pretty quickly a class's level of internal familiarity and act accordingly. In a class with high internal familiarity, students will likely be talking with each other as they arrive. There will be relationships, inside jokes, an established culture, and some level of existing internal rapport that the librarian would do well to tap into it. Zoller and Landry recommend identifying the person who is the "point of origin," if possible.[3] This is the person who influences the group, perhaps through humor, gregariousness, or charm. Adversely, this point of origin may also set a tone for the group that is negative, skeptical, and vocally disinterested. Either way, the librarian wants to establish rapport with this person, as doing so will likely bring the class along.

Use the Time before Class, As Students Arrive, to Set a Friendly and Welcoming Tone

Smile and greet students as they come in. Make small talk. In Wisconsin, we often rely on the weather as the basis for small talk, but even asking, "How's your day going so far?" can get students talking. Subtly listening in on conversations students are having among themselves before class—if they don't seem too personal—can offer the librarian an opportunity to connect. This can be an effective way for the librarian to get to know students, even a little. If students are talking about the class, for example, this might be a perfect opportunity for the librarian to express an interest and even begin to suggest how the day's session will help.

We often use this preclass time to check in with an early arriving student about the assignment at hand and assess the preparedness of the students. Have they been introduced to the research assignment? Have they selected topics? Often other students will chime in on this casual chat about the assignment. The more the librarian knows about the assignment and the students' understanding of and concerns about it, the better she can position herself as an ally ready to help. The librarian should, however, guard against taking the role of ally too far. Sometimes these preclass chats about the assignment can result in students complaining about the assignment, the class, or even the instructor. The librarian will want to tread carefully here, not wanting to be perceived as "taking sides" with a disgruntled student against the instructor.

In our library we have experimented with having PowerPoint slideshows running as the students come in. The slideshow contains trivia questions, humor, and information about the library, and as students guess at an answer or react to the slides, interaction among students and librarian is likely to occur. This can be an effective strategy with a low-internal-familiarity group as it's a common experience that can subtly bring them together.

Your body language can help establish rapport without taking any extra time. Standard public-speaking tips, like smiling, making eye contact, using natural but varied facial expressions and gestures, and moving around can all make you seem more relaxed, more approachable, and more engaged with your students.

Look for Hooks

Sales people and public speakers recognize that identifying what they have in common with their clients, audience, or—in the case of librarians—students is an effective method of establishing rapport. Sometimes these elements of commonality can be identified during the preclass banter. "I know! It was so cold my eyelashes froze shut on the walk to work this morning" or "Did anyone else stay up way too late watching the Olympics last night?" Be aware that strategies for finding commonalities may evolve over the course of your career. If, for example, you are a recently graduated librarian, you may have a much stronger connection to students and student life than a librarian who has been in the field for many years. As your situation diverges, in age and/or experience, from that of your students, you may have to look for similarities elsewhere; for example, "My daughter and her roommate have different ideas about the division of social time and study time in their dorm room. If you are having the same issue, keep in mind that the library offers spaces for both."

Use Names . . . Theirs, if Possible, and Yours

Introduce yourself. Librarians usually don't have the time to learn and remember the names of all the students in a one-shot session. However, even using some of the students' names can build rapport with the entire group. When calling on a student, ask his or her name, and then use it again later in the session. Sometimes this can effectively be done with a student identified as a "point of origin," who has already displayed an affinity for attention and who has attained a certain social standing in the group. Another alternative is to have students write their first names on folded index cards set out as nameplates for the duration of the class. The librarian can then call on them by name.

Be Authentic

In a typical one-shot scenario, a librarian is facing a room full of strangers, being observed by the disciplinary colleague, without knowing how well the students have been prepared for the session. It can be a stressful situation, and it is easy to put up one's defenses, intentionally or not, and come across as stiff, pedantic, scripted, or boring. If insecurity crops up, combat it with an antidote of humility and honesty. Become comfortable with saying, "I don't know. Let's find out." One of our librarians describes himself as a terrible speller. He routinely asks students how to spell things during class and talks about how unforgiving some databases can be for bad spellers. This openness puts the students at ease and engages them as they helped identify and correct the spelling errors. In another situation, a librarian was asked to teach an accounting class. Having very little background in accounting jargon and concepts, she openly admitted to the students and the instructor that she would be relying on their subject expertise in conducting searches and assessing results. Modeling and explaining that we each come to the table with different skill sets and areas of expertise, and that bringing them together yields the best results eases the pressure on the students, the librarian, and the instructor. It acknowledges that they each have something to offer, but no one has to feel like they need to "know everything." The librarian can build trust among students by exuding the kind of confidence that is not based on already knowing all the answers.

Tell Stories

People connect with stories, and librarians have a lot to tell. One librarian likes to include at least one story in every instruction session that begins with "A student came to the reference desk the other day looking for . . ." or "I was working with a student on her research project about . . ." The students in the class visibly become more engaged upon hearing these phrases. Suddenly this librarian is telling a story about another student, someone with whom the students can relate, someone who was struggling with a research problem. And the story goes on to say how this student was helped by the librarian.

Consider these two examples. The librarian could say, "Sometimes you have to think of another way to ask a question to be able to search it effectively." Or the librarian could say, "The other day a student came to the reference desk and her research topic was 'What's good about mosquitoes?' She was not finding anything. Go figure! What *is* good about mosquitoes?" After the requisite "Nothing" response, and agreeing that we all hate mosquitoes, a student suggests that they provide food for other forms of life. "So how might we translate that into a search?" "Mosquitoes and food chain," responds another student. "Yes!" responds the librarian. "Sometimes you have to approach the question differently and try to anticipate possible answers to the question." This small lesson became more meaningful, memorable, and interactive with the help of a brief story.

FACILITATING MEANINGFUL DISCUSSION

Throughout this book we have advocated the shift toward active learning strategies for librarians. Central to the active learning instruction sessions described in this book is the ability to lead meaningful discussions. The professional pedagogy literature is replete with resources on active learning strategies and techniques for instructors. However, it does not often deal with the unique circumstances in which teaching librarians find themselves. Most of the literature assumes a semester- or year-long relationship with students, and therefore a luxury of time not usually available to librarians. Still, there is much to be gleaned from this literature.

One of the most challenging aspects of transitioning from a lecture- and demonstration-based teaching style to one emphasizing discovery and discussion is the ability to get students actively engaged in meaningful discussion. Librarians know that asking questions is key to getting a discussion going, but what do you do when no one answers? How do you ask questions that prompt more than a nod? How do you make a discussion interesting, informative, and interactive? Books on using discussion in teaching suggest that instructors prepare students for discussion by doing things like establishing ground rules, modeling discussions (perhaps with a group of other instructors), clarifying the importance of discussion in the syllabus and through the grading structure of the class, getting to know their students, promoting civility and community among students, and building trust and rapport with their students.[4] Clearly, librarians are not in a position to put all of these suggestions into play, but there are steps they can take to address some of these issues within the confines of their limited time with students.

Don't Blindside the Students

Along with building rapport, it is important for the librarian to establish trust and a sense of a safe environment to encourage participation. For this reason, it is a good idea not to put students on the spot to answer a question, especially at the beginning of a class when they have not yet had the opportunity to figure you out, to sense how you will react to a response, and to know if it will be "safe" (i.e., not embarrassing or humiliating) to risk a response to your questions. Zoller and Landry suggest "foreshadowing" as a technique for preparing students to answer a question.[5] This strategy lets students know ahead of time what you will be asking them, thus removing the threat of being surprised or blindsided by a question they weren't expecting. A librarian may say, "As you look at your search results, think about what makes some of the results more appealing to you than other ones. We will share these observations when we come back together." The librarian can employ this foreshadowing technique in another way as he observes and assists individual students and groups during their independent exploration time. The librarian may help a group of students with a research question that exemplifies a common experience. He can foreshadow by saying, "When we get back together as a group for discussion, this would be a great example to share with the rest of the class." At the point in the discussion where it seems appropriate to share this experience, the students may voluntarily offer to share their experience. If not, a little gentle prompting from the librarian is likely to encourage them to share: "This group had an interesting dilemma. Would you care to share what you found?" Through foreshadowing, the group has been prepared to participate in the conversation and given the confidence that they have something worthwhile to contribute.

Be an Active Listener

Be conscious of how you respond to students. It is not about making you look good but about making the student look good. Well-known *Washington Post* columnist E. J. Dionne spoke at our campus several years ago. One thing that stood out about his presentation was the way he handled the students' questions afterward. Students worked up the nerve to approach a microphone in front of a packed auditorium to ask a question of this world-class journalist, who earned his fame in part by asking really good questions. Dionne made every student look good. He did this by treating each student with the utmost respect and dignity, thanking them for posing the question, and practicing active listening techniques. He made eye contact and nodded in understanding as they spoke. He considered their questions, sometimes by pausing before responding. He paraphrased questions to ensure he was understanding what they were asking, and he followed up with further questions, turning the question into a conversation. Librarians can practice these same techniques.

Ask Specific but Open-Ended Questions

Questions that can be answered with yes or no tend not to go anywhere. The librarian asks the class after a period of independent searching, "Did you find anything?" Students nod yes. The discussion ceases until the librarian asks another question. In one lesson, we have students describe their research topics to partners who in turn are tasked with trying to find a good source for that research topic. After this partner activity, the librarian brings the group back as a whole for discussion. Invariably when the librarian begins this discussion with a question like "Well, how did that go?" the discussion falls flat. The question is open ended but too vague to elicit a response. The students don't know what the librarian is looking for and may not yet feel the emotional safety required to take a chance on answering the question. If, however, the librarian says something like "Who would like to give a shout-out to their partner for finding a really good source?" the discussion usually takes flight. It's a nonthreatening question, focusing on something positive, and also a little lighthearted. A student will usually respond.

Ask Clarifying Questions

This might be a question that asks the student to dig a little deeper by providing more evidence, explanation, or example. For instance, in the previous scenario when a student responds to the question by indicating that his partner has found a really good source, a clarifying question might be "What makes it good?" Whenever possible, don't let students get away with the easy response; challenge them to take it one step further. Sometimes a simple "Tell me more" or "Say more" is enough to elicit a more thoughtful and developed response from a student. When possible, challenge the student to reach a little further by asking a follow-up question rather than letting them off the hook with a "Good job" or "Yes." Follow-up questions can be opened up for response by the rest of the class, so that the original respondent doesn't feel "punished" for participating.

Ask Questions to Which You Don't Already Have Answers

For authentic discussion, avoid the tactic of having students guess what you are thinking. They know when this is happening, and the risk of giving the "wrong" answer is enough to shut down participation among all but the most intrepid students. Avoid the lecture question, the one that says, "I don't really want to know what you think; I want you all to know what I think, but I'm framing it as a question."

Connect Student Contributions

When possible, ask questions that put students in conversation with each other rather than with you. "Jake just said that one of the drawbacks of Wikipedia is that anyone can edit it. But Kelsey suggests that that is one of the things that makes it powerful. Jake, how do you respond to that?" Another strategy for encouraging students to engage with each other is to give students the opportunity to respond to another student's question rather than answering it yourself. For example, if a student asks, "What does 'peer reviewed' mean," turn it over to the class to see if another student has an answer.

Get Comfortable with Silence

What instructor, especially new instructors or those in an unfamiliar group, doesn't dread dead silence in response to a question? Librarians are almost always in front of an unfamiliar group and often lament the silent stares of seemingly disinterested students. Silence is often required as students process a question and prepare to answer it. If the silence becomes uncomfortable, often a student will speak, if for no other reason than to ease the discomfort. This student's boldness should be rewarded, with a positive response or a "thank you" from the librarian. We have experienced situations where the silence persists and action must be taken. It's almost as if there were a statute of limitations for responding to a question, and if it passes, it is almost an unspoken rule that a student cannot then break it, or he or she is somehow breaking ranks with the group. Such a silence may indicate a problem with the question or imply that rapport has not yet been adequately established to provide a sense of safety for the students. In this case, avoid answering your own question. It sends a signal to the students that you already have the answer you are looking for and will provide it if they remain silent long enough. It also lets them know that if they wait long enough, they will be able to spend much of the session passively listening as you fill in the blanks for them. Rather, rephrase the question. Offering a more specific question, one with clearer parameters, may give students surer footing on which to risk an answer. For example, if the question "What do you need to know about the library to complete your assignment" elicits no responses, you might rephrase it: "Who can start us off by telling me one thing you need to do with this assignment?" By asking for just one low-risk response, you can prime the pump of student conversation. Your response will be positive and encouraging, thus developing a "safe" environment for students to participate in as your questions build in complexity.

WHEN THE BEST LAID PLANS OF
MICE AND MEN GO AWRY

We have suggested strategies for facilitating discussions that focus on the students and the librarian. However, most library one-shot sessions include another player: the course instructor. The presence of the instructor adds another dimension to the session, again contributing to the uniqueness of the teaching situation that librarians encounter. Ideally, the course instructor is an ally, someone who can be instrumental in establishing rapport by presenting the librarian as a trusted colleague and by encouraging students to participate in discussions. But sometimes a well-meaning instructor can inadvertently derail a library session.

Instructor Answers Questions Meant for Students

That uncomfortable silence we discussed earlier can be even more uncomfortable to the course instructor, who feels somewhat responsible for the students' behavior with a "guest presenter." Embarrassed by the students' reluctance to participate, an instructor might alleviate this discomfort by responding to librarian questions directed to the students. How does the librarian handle this situation? It may be helpful to dig into that bag of facilitating-discussions tricks. Perhaps the librarian can redirect the conversation by asking a student to respond to what the instructor has said, or to provide an example of what the instructor has said. "Your instructor has just defined what 'peer reviewed' means for us. Who thinks they might have found an example of an article from a peer-reviewed journal?" If the instructor persists in answering questions, the librarian may take slightly more direct approaches, such as, "Let's hear from this side of the room," or good-naturedly saying, "I know that your professor has strong feelings about this, but I want to hear from you this time."

Instructor Derails the Lesson

Another all-too-common situation brought about by the well-intentioned instructor is the impromptu request for instruction that deviates substantially from the plan. You have carefully planned your session ahead of time, ideally in consultation with the instructor, discussing what you will cover in your limited time with the students. Then, as the lesson unfolds, the instructor says, "Oh, could you also go over citing sources in APA style and using EndNote?" Internally the librarian may be saying, "No, I can't! I only have 50 minutes!" but externally the librarian must summon her most diplomatic countenance. She may be able to address the point in a cursory manner, giving a brief overview of what APA is or what EndNote is, and then refer the class to online resources for more information. The librarian may couch her response as, "Though it would take more time than we have available to us today to really get into this, let me refer you to some resources that can help." This may be an opportune time for the librarian to invite students to her office hours or to the reference desk for one-on-one assistance. Depending on the relationship that the librarian has with the instructor, she may even say, "We could spend another session looking at that. I'd be happy to come back and cover that with you." You will want to be sensitive to the possibility that the instructor is suggesting this alternative direction because she is not finding the current direction useful for her students. While this may be difficult for the librarian to consider, one way to address this possibility is for the librarian to offer the instructor a choice. "OK, we were planning to spend the next 20 minutes exploring some specialized databases. But if you prefer, we can instead look at EndNote." This signals to the instructor that you can't do it all, and if they would rather go in a different direction, you are willing to do that.

Instructor Doesn't Show Up, or Leaves

While the previous scenarios depict situations in which an instructor's presence can pose challenges for teaching librarians, an arguably greater challenge is when the instructor doesn't show up at all. We believe it's important to have a policy on instructor presence for library instruction sessions. Such a policy will protect librarians from those thinly veiled "substitute-teaching" requests to meet with a class when the professor is going to be away at a conference or otherwise unable to meet with a class. Some argue that these situations, though not ideal, are still an opportunity for librarians to get face time with students and are better than nothing. We prefer to require instructor attendance at these sessions, as our experience demonstrates that students are much less engaged when their instructors are not there, instructor participation in the session sends a strong message to the students about the importance of the session, and the synergy created by the presence of both the librarian and the instructor better serves the needs of the students and the research task at hand. If questions come up about the assignment, the instructor can address them, clarifying expectations for both the students and the librarian. Some library instruction policies, in addition to stating their expectation that the instructor be present for the session, even go so far as to state that the librarian reserves the right to cancel the session if the instructor is not present. We recommend carefully weighing the potential political fallout of doing so before invoking this option.

Class Is Unprepared

In previous chapters we have emphasized the importance of having students come to the session prepared with a research topic and in some cases having completed prerequisites or preparatory activities to make the library session more productive. However, even with carefully communicated expectations and preparations, things don't always go as planned and students don't always arrive to class prepared.

As any instructor—or student—knows, sometimes a class does not adhere to its syllabus. As a result, a class may show up for a library instruction session on a pre-scheduled date, but they haven't covered the material they had expected to cover by this time. Students may come to class not yet having selected a research topic or not yet having been introduced to their upcoming research assignment. Or perhaps the students were to have arrived having completed a prerequisite such as developing a concept map to narrow their topics or having done preliminary background research, but they haven't. The librarian only learns this during preclass banter with students or the instructor. Librarians are in a unique teaching situation in that they have little control over what happens in a class outside of their instruction session. They have to be ready to improvise in any teaching situation. Librarians are encouraged to keep a toolbox of backup plans—lessons that they can pull into service when the students aren't prepared for the lesson designed for them. These backup plans may be nothing more than ideas that the librarian has tucked away in his mind, or they may be more developed and fixed in an online or print format. The librarian's toolbox of backup plans should contain a collection of a la carte items that can be selected and combined to best meet the needs of the students in any given situation. While such an on-the-fly, improvised class may not be as optimal as a carefully and thoughtfully constructed lesson, it can nonetheless be effective, especially the more practiced and adept the librarian is at using the various tools.

These are examples of a la carte instruction activities that we keep in our toolboxes:

- *Concept mapping*: Present a short video demonstrating a concept mapping exercise. This can be supplemented by an introduction to reference tools for finding background information on a topic. This activity can be useful when students arrive without having a research topic in mind.

Source: UWEC Photography

- *Working with a collection of "generic" research topics likely to appeal to students*: By having some timely topic ideas at hand that are likely to appeal to students, we can let students select one to practice the research skills they will be learning. Examples of topics we have used recently include voter ID laws and college students, college student loan debt, sexual assault on college campuses, mining, and tobacco-use policies on college campuses.
- *Topic shopping*: Students can try out topics they are considering for their project.
- *Working from a required reading*: Starting from a required reading for the course, such as an article on e-reserve or chapter from their textbook, we can introduce students to the ideas of citation chasing and joining an intellectual conversation. They can use that reading with which they are familiar as a jumping-off point for finding related sources or following a conversation.
- *Reviewing preselected sources on a topic*: Similar to the idea of having timely topics at the ready, we also keep collections of online links to a variety of source types relating to a single topic. Resources might include a scholarly article, an infographic, an online video, a social media site with user-generated content, a newspaper article, and an e-book. Students can review these sources in groups and discuss why the source was created, when and how they would use such a resource, and how it is in conversation with other sources.
- *Explore the physical reference collection*: Take students to the reference collection to have them investigate how encyclopedias can be pathways into research.

Technology Poses Challenges

Who has not had the experience of being in front of a class only to have technology fail spectacularly? The campus system is down. The Internet connection is down. Or the teaching station went up in smoke—literally. Sometimes it's a technical malfunction that happens before or during a session. Sometimes the technology challenge is not the result of a malfunction but rather an unanticipated or unfamiliar space or less-than-ideal technology setup. For example, maybe you are teaching a specialized database for which your campus has only single-user access (and it's not possible to add multiuser access for training purposes). Or maybe you are teaching in a lab on campus that has group computer stations but no teaching station.

Or perhaps one section of your first-year composition course is taught at a distance, with students spread out among multiple locations, so the partner activity you normally employ is not possible. Again, it is useful for the librarian to have a section of the toolbox for these kinds of contingencies. Added to the toolbox above are strategies such as the following:

- *Letting a student do the driving*: If you are in a teaching situation where there is only one computer, like the teaching station in a traditional classroom, or you are in a situation where only a single log-on is allowed, just one person will be

Source: UWEC Photography

able to search at a time. Why not have it be a student? Invite a student or a small group of students to the teaching station, and let the others play the role of backseat driver, offering advice and telling the student(s) at the wheel what to do. Students are much more likely to engage with and help out a peer than they are a librarian in the driver's seat. Similarly, if you are in a distance-education situation, where students are scattered at multiple locations and connected only by technology, try using one student's research topic as an example and have the others contribute ideas to help this student. They are then dealing with a "real" situation and are more likely to contribute ideas to help another student than to respond to a hypothetical research need.

- *Use imposed groupings to your advantage*: If you have a situation where students are divided into groups, such as gathered around a single computer in a group workstation setting, or divided between an on-campus and a distant site, use these imposed group settings to the class's advantage. Perhaps each group will evaluate a particular resource or finding tool. Then they can come together to compare and contrast what they have found. You can even introduce some good-natured competition. Maybe each group has to "sell" their database or their article. What does it have that the other group's artifact does not have?
- *Keep a bank of short demonstration videos on hand for backup*: It is not unusual to experience a short, temporary outage of a particular search tool at precisely the time you need it. The catalog is acting up. A particular database just hiccupped. Though not ideal or interactive, short videos demonstrating the tool can be useful backup mechanisms that at the very least demonstrate the basics of a tool, and sometimes buy enough time for the problem to be resolved!
- *Keep a collection of print artifacts for teaching evaluation*: Print out several types of resources, such as scholarly articles, websites, infographics, newspaper articles, and so on, on a topic. When technology lets you down, paper can be your friend. Have students travel from one artifact to another responding to evaluation questions for each. Your library may want to keep several such files on hand, each on a different topic, so that it is more likely that you will have one that will be of interest and relevant to any given class. Be sure to review these files from time to time to ensure that the topics and the artifacts are still relevant and likely to be of interest to students.
- *Consider rescheduling*: If technology malfunctions present an insurmountable hurdle to teaching the lesson you had planned, maybe it's better to cut your losses and schedule another session. Or is there an alternative but still valuable lesson you can quickly insert? This is a decision you will likely have to make in consultation with the instructor.
- *Be nimble with teaching spaces*: If technological problems or scheduling conflicts preclude you from using your primary teaching space, do you have backup options? Our library purchased a set of 30 iPads to expand our teaching options beyond our single computer lab. Not only has the iPad lab enabled us to better accommodate requests for instruction at times conducive to curricular needs by

turning any classroom or space into a hands-on teaching lab, but it has helped us out in jams. When computer equipment hasn't worked, or when our single lab has been inadvertently double booked, we were able to pull in the iPads to the rescue. Of course, purchasing a set of iPads, or laptops or other devices, is not always an option. However, the librarian should familiarize herself with other teaching space and technology options on campus. On our campus, that means becoming familiar with other general-access labs and the policies for using and reserving them. Cultivating strong relationships with other departments, as we have advocated in previous chapters, offers an additional benefit if they have a collection of laptops or mobile devices, or a special-purpose lab that they are willing to let you use in a pinch. On some campuses, students typically carry laptops or tablets to class, providing another alternative.

What all of these situations have in common is that the librarian really doesn't know what to expect. As a result, librarians must be ready to improvise. The prepared librarian would do well to work through these scenarios as what-if situations, developing backup plans to have in place and in mind should an unexpected situation arise. Librarians may want to use these what-if situations as discussion topics at staff or professional development meetings, sharing ideas for and experiences in handling unexpected or difficult teaching situations. The more tools that the librarian keeps in an improvisation tool kit, the better equipped she will be to deal with whatever situation arises to rescue that one shot.

NOTES

1. "Building Rapport," in *Brilliant Public Speaking*, Career Library.TV video, from Films on Demand, 4:30, 2010, http://digital.films.com/PortalPlaylists.aspx?aid=4552&xtid=53231.
2. Kendall Zoller and Claudette Landry, *The Choreography of Presenting: The 7 Essential Abilities of Effective Presenters* (Thousand Oaks, CA: Corwin Press, 2010), 62.
3. Ibid., 60.
4. Stephen D. Brookfield and Stephen Preskill, *Discussion as a Way of Teaching: Tools and Techniques for Democratic Classrooms* (San Francisco: Jossey-Bass, 2005), 42–62; C. Roland Christensen, David A. Garvin, and Ann Sweet, *Education for Judgment: The Artistry of Discussion Leadership* (Boston: Harvard Business School Press, 1991), 15–34.
5. Zoller and Landry, *The Choreography of Presenting*, 75.

10

Interviewing the "Others"

What the Disciplinary Faculty Said

One of the key components of our process was involving disciplinary faculty in the revision process. Not only did this partnership strengthen our relationships with the faculty and enhance our knowledge of their curriculum, but it also increased buy-in for the success and continued reassessment of the resulting one-shot lessons.

But it turns out the benefits of our collaborations didn't just go one way. In this chapter we interview several of the faculty we have worked with during the past five years. We include remarks from two of the English faculty who participated in the first-year composition one-shot revision, three nursing faculty who worked on the multicourse project, and the director of our campus's Center for Excellence in Teaching and Learning (CETL) who facilitated the Lesson Studies. All but the three nurses, who chose to share a conversation transcribed by Jonathan Pumper, were interviewed over e-mail.

Cathy Rex, associate professor of English
Participant in the First-Year Composition One-Shot Revision through Lesson Study (LS)
Cathy Rex is an associate professor of English at the University of Wisconsin–Eau Claire. Her research and teaching interests include race and gender in early America with a special focus on texts by and about women writers, Native American writers, and early American material and visual culture (gubernatorial seals, portraiture, money, tombstones, etc.). Her work has appeared in *American Quarterly*, *Women's Studies*, and *College & Research Libraries*. Her book *Anglo-American Women Writers and Representations of Indianness, 1629–1824* is forthcoming from Ashgate Publishing.

Lesson Study required a significant investment of your time and energy. What made you commit to being involved in the process?

Figure 10.1.   Cathy Rex. *UWEC Photography*

Honestly, my initial reason for joining the Lesson Study [LS] process was because of the people involved. I knew and respected all of the library and English faculty who were participating, and I knew that because of those people, the project would be a successful one in the long run. There is nothing like knowing you're betting on a "sure thing" from the outset; that had huge appeal. The small stipend we received for our participation and the publication/presentation/scholarly development potential of the LS project were also huge draws for me—at least at first.

Once I was actively immersed in the LS, however, I could see bigger and more meaningful outcomes that fueled my involvement in and excitement for the project—namely, the opportunities for interdisciplinary collaboration and the chance to improve a troubling aspect of most freshman-level writing classes: the one-shot research lesson. I realized that through this LS, I was in a position to improve nearly every single student's experience on the University of Wisconsin–Eau Claire campus as well as enhance the relationship and collaboration between English and library faculty. These layers of "enticement"—the initial draw of a stipend and excellent collaborators and then the allure of making real, substantial changes in pedagogy—made the time and energy investment in the LS especially meaningful for me.

Describe your experience with the one-shot library instruction session (both before and after collaboration).

Although I worked with an excellent librarian (Eric Jennings) prior to the LS experience, I think that both my students and I found the one-shot library sessions to be ancillary to what we were doing in our writing classes. The library sessions seemed like a "ticket punch" moment that the students were required to go through in order to move on in their writing classes, and I felt obligated to help them acquire that ticket punch. During these one-shot sessions (prior to the LS), the students inevitably felt like they were taught things they already knew and were more interested in beginning their own research, checking Facebook, or surfing the Internet, instead of paying attention to the one-shot lesson. I always felt like it was a wasted opportunity for the students to actually learn to use the library and its many resources. This is in no way a criticism of Eric or any of the librarians I have worked with over the years (both at UW–Eau Claire and elsewhere), but more a comment on the problematic nature of the one-shot lesson, on the poor communication that often exists between library faculty and faculty in other disciplines who request the one-shots, and on the misconception held by most faculty that library professors are "miracle workers" who can cover everything in a 50-minute one-shot.

After the LS experience, I view things very differently. Not only do I now have a better understanding of what librarians can and can't do for students, but I feel I am better able to communicate with library faculty about what my students in a particular class need from the one-shot lesson. I also feel I am a better university citizen and have a much clearer understanding of what my librarian colleagues face in these one-shots and how complex teaching research—especially in 50 minutes— can be. As a consequence, I work with more intentionality to prepare my students for these one-shot library sessions. Prior to the LS, I think I viewed the one-shots as self-contained, self-explanatory supplements to my classes. Now, I view them as an integral part of my classes that I intentionally scaffold my assignments toward and consistently reference throughout the term. The one-shot is now, truly, a central, deliberate part of my freshman writing classes, whereas before it was admittedly an add-on.

What outcomes have you observed as a result of this collaboration?

In terms of my own teaching and collegiality, I have, as I've mentioned previously, become a more conscious and informed university citizen. I have a better understanding of what librarians do and a better sense of the complexity of teaching "research" from their perspective. I also think I have become a better communicator with library faculty and my own students. For example, I now have a better grasp of all of the steps that go into finding and vetting a source and the complexities of relaying that to students. Of course, I "knew" how to research and understood that it is a complex process before the LS—I am an English professor who researches and writes for a living, after all—but I think I had forgotten how many steps and decisions go into the process of finding and evaluating a source as well as the difficulties of relaying that information to students. All of that has become second nature to me as a skilled researcher with years of experience. The LS forced me to peel back the layers of my own cache of knowledge to see all of the intricate steps, skills, and information students needed to be taught in order to become more comfortable with and competent at source gathering.

What was most challenging about this collaboration?

I think the most challenging aspect of this collaboration would be the long, drawn-out nature of the Lesson Study process. Because of the schedules of the various faculty participants, campus holidays, and breaks, the fact that the one-shot is only taught at one particular point in each semester—at least at UW–Eau Claire it occurs at a specific point in the Blugold Seminar schedule—and the nature of Lesson Study itself, this collaboration spanned multiple semesters, and, at times, it was hard to maintain the initial momentum and excitement of the process.

Figure 10.2. Shevaun E. Watson.
UWEC Photography

Shevaun Watson, associate professor of English and director of the University Writing Program

Participant in the First-Year Composition One-Shot Revision through Lesson Study (LS)

Shevaun E. Watson is associate professor of English and director of the University Writing Program (the Blugold Seminar in Critical Reading and Writing). She has been teaching college composition for more than 15 years in a variety of institutional settings. In her role as Writing Program Administrator (WPA) at UW–Eau Claire, she provides instructional support and faculty development for all Blugold Seminar instructors, develops curriculum, and assesses program outcomes. Shevaun is also the primary contact on campus for writing-across-the-curriculum (WAC) and writing-in-the-disciplines (WID) initiatives and concerns. Shevaun is an award-winning scholar in writing studies, focusing on relationships between curriculum and student learning (e.g., transfer; stereotype threat). Her research interests also include African American literacies and rhetorics, transatlanticism, and public memory. Her work has appeared in *College Composition and Communication, Rhetoric Society Quarterly, Writing Program Administration, Rhetorica, Early American Literature, Writing Center Journal, Composition Studies, College & Research Libraries*, and five edited collections.

Lesson Study required a significant investment of your time and energy. What made you commit to being involved in the process?

I knew that I didn't know a lot about information literacy, teaching research, or what collegiate librarians know and do. And I knew that these gaps in my understanding potentially hindered my ability to be an effective Writing Program Administrator [WPA]. I attended a professional development workshop offered by Kate Hinnant on teaching research in first-year composition, and I came away from that knowing I needed to know a lot more about this stuff. Also, as a brand-new WPA then [2009], I was highly motivated to build any kind of relationships and collaborations across campus that I could, so this seemed like an excellent opportunity to do that. Finally, I really liked and respected the people involved in the project; that made a big difference, too, in my initial motivation and my level of engagement all the way through.

Describe your experience with the one-shot library instruction session (both before and after collaboration).

Before the collaboration on the Lesson Study and the development of a new one-shot session, I found the library instruction to be "unsatisfying" or "incomplete" but in ways that I couldn't articulate—to myself, to my students, or to library faculty. I knew it was important and valued the information that the librarians were providing during the session, and I tried to make it meaningful and relevant for my students. I tried to time it right with our work in class, for example, but still the students didn't seem to get much out of it. Very little carried over to their research skills or research writing—or at least very little that was clearly discernible. The main reason I did the library instruction session at that point was to get the students physically in the library, but I don't know if the session even achieved that goal of making students more familiar and comfortable with the library as a major resource on campus. The "research paper" has long been a problem in first-year composition as something that is often required or expected of the course, but also as something that is very hard to teach and get students to do well. The library session at this point just seemed like part of a larger problem: something's wrong here, but I don't know how to go about fixing it.

After the collaboration on the Lesson Study project, my experience of the one-shot session is entirely different. First, I have a much better understanding of librarians' perspectives and areas of expertise. The Lesson Study provided me with a fairly deep understanding—or "deep" for someone outside of the field—of the complexities of information literacy, information organization and access, and information technologies. That alone helps me make the session more useful and relevant to my students because I see the "bigger picture" behind the one-shot session; I see now how I can work as a conduit or liaison between the library and my students' research needs. I had such a simplistic and "functional" view of information literacy prior to the Lesson Study, which greatly impeded my ability to be that conduit, to make the connections, to bridge the gap, as it were, for my students. Because I now recognize and rely on my colleagues' expertise in this area, I no longer see the one-shot session as a one-time "inoculation" of researching skills that students need, but rather as the beginning of a process, of a conversation, of a way of thinking that will continue for both me and my students.

Second, my views of the one-shot session were changed as a result of our collaboration on the Lesson Study because I became aware of the variety of institutional constraints and demands under which library faculty work. Before then, I was completely ignorant about the "service" and "basic skills" mentality that dominated librarians' work with other faculty across campus. I admit that I saw myself in this as they talked about the unrealistic and idiosyncratic—and even at times offensive or patronizing—expectations and views of colleagues "in the disciplines." Furthermore, I think we came to understand that, in this regard, there was a great deal of common ground and shared experiences among us. First-year writing, too, is widely seen as a "service course" that teaches students "basic skills" on college campuses (that they wouldn't need if K–12 education "did its job") and is therefore not highly regarded by other faculty. During the Lesson Study, we came to understand these common misperceptions that often played a large role in our day-to-day work with students and faculty. An understanding of this shared position motivated me to see the one-shot lessons as more of a collaboration and mutual investment than mere instruction in functional research skills.

What outcomes have you observed as a result of this collaboration?

1. Increased understanding between the library/library faculty and the composition program/composition faculty.
2. A stronger composition program and curriculum overall.
3. A shared language around information literacy learning.
4. Reciprocal gains: the library faculty taught me about information literacy; I helped them understand rhetoric. Both were mutually beneficial.
5. New professional commitment to advocating for the important role that information literacy plays in a first-year writing course and program.

What does this look like? The library faculty are now integrally involved in the development and assessment of relevant components of the first-year writing curriculum. They offer insights and expertise on the information literacy learning outcomes and instructional resources for the course. They are reading student work from the course along with composition faculty to help create and undertake assessment of information literacy learning. We are all equally invested in understanding students' learning and finding ways to support and improve it. The library faculty also play a major role in the professional-development components of the composition program. In this role, they not only provide writing faculty with teaching resources and practical support, they also give the information literacy parts of the course some real intellectual and scholarly weight. This creates more buy-in among composition faculty, especially as they can see that we're all on the same page. As the WPA, I rely on this collaboration a great deal; it's becomes absolutely integral to the program and to my overall effectiveness as the program leader. I have a much deeper professional interest in the role of information literacy in first-year writing programs overall. I now read scholarship in the area of this overlap and see myself contributing to it in the future. I have become somewhat of a convert to the importance of information literacy learning in a writing course and feel committed to developing that as a larger theme of my professional identity and work.

What was most challenging about this collaboration?

The greatest challenge was at the beginning of the Lesson Study process. It took weeks and weeks of discussion and some debate to even begin to get on the same page in terms of what we wanted as a shared goal of the project. Words and phrases that one group perceived as obvious were completely unfamiliar to the other: *rheto-*

ric, rhetorical situation, exigence, ethos, complexity, evidence, source type, information cycle, citation chasing, literacy, and so on. All of these needed to be explained, illustrated, and integrated into our working vocabulary.

Another challenge was objectively observing and assessing the lesson itself. It was difficult to gauge students' understanding during the lesson and after. Multiple factors could explain students' comments and questions during the lesson and in the debriefing session afterward. So we needed to talk through various explanations and possibilities and come to some agreement about what to focus on, what to fix, and how to go about doing that. Refining the lesson to meet specific objectives, even through the structure process of a Lesson Study, is difficult to achieve when so many people and factors are involved in the lesson itself.

Provide perspective from your role as the composition director and the intersection of this work with the development of the Blugold Seminar.

The opportunity for the Lesson Study preceded my undertaking a full-scale revision of the first-year writing program, so my involvement in the Lesson Study at that early stage deeply impacted my thinking about ways that the composition program could be improved. The timing worked incredibly well for both me as WPA and for the library faculty because they were in on the eventual revamping of the program from the ground up. Library colleagues were not mere consultants on course outcomes and instructional resources but became integral stakeholders in the curriculum overall and played a defining role in conceptualizing parts of the new course. The library involvement in the program is one of its defining features and is something I greatly value and rely upon. There are, of course, many composition programs and many university libraries working separately and together to improve students' information literacy learning. But I do think that the experience of the Lesson Study put us on a slightly different, and better, path—one that yielded open communication, mutual respect, scholarly collaborations, intellectual conversations, and ongoing partnerships.

Arin VanWormer, assistant professor of nursing
Angie Stombaugh, associate professor of nursing
Rita Sperstad, assistant professor of nursing
Participants in the Three-Year Nursing One-Shot Revision through Lesson Study

Arin VanWormer is an assistant professor in the College of Nursing at the University of Wisconsin–Eau Claire. In addition to teaching, she works with nursing students in a variety of programs. In her faculty role, Arin coordinates a seven-credit capstone course and works with undergraduate student nurses in the clinical setting. Similarly, she works with completion and graduate students in the didactic setting and on independent research and scholarly projects. Arin continuously pursues curricular improvements and development, seeks novel ways to improve organizational communication, and assesses program outcomes. She participates in

Figure 10.3.   The Nursing Lesson Study Team. *UWEC Photography*

professional committees within the university and with institutions and agencies in the surrounding community. Arin has led and collaborated with various research teams that have published in alternative and integrative therapies, telemedicine, interdisciplinary collaboration, and information literacy.

Rita Sperstad is an assistant professor in the College of Nursing at the University of Wisconsin–Eau Claire. As a professional nurse, Rita has developed three main areas of scholarship: she has a specialty in maternity nursing practice; research and coordination of equity, diversity, and inclusivity in nursing; and is passionate about using active teaching strategies to promote engaged learning. Rita teaches in the undergraduate, graduate, and the RN-to-BSN completion programs. She chairs the Nursing Honors Program, personally facilitating several nursing students with an interest in labor and birth as their honors topic area. Rita's research has focused on cultural transformation in practicing nurses, team-based learning in undergraduate teaching, and the Lesson Study model to teach information- and evidence-based practice skills to nursing students.

Angie Stombaugh is an associate professor in the College of Nursing and the director of the Center for Excellence in Teaching and Learning (CETL) at the University of Wisconsin–Eau Claire. In her faculty role, Angie teaches professional aspects of nursing to undergraduates and advance practice nursing—specifically pediatrics—in the doctoral program. In her director's role, Angie creates and coordinates programming for faculty on campus to advance teaching using best practices to engage students in the classroom. Programming has focused on online-teaching best practices, active learning in the classroom, and designing engaging classrooms, courses, and curriculum. Angie's research interests include lesson planning for student engagement, admission requirements for success in the nursing program, information literacy, and interdisciplinary collaboration.

Lesson Study required a significant investment of your time and energy. What made you commit to being involved in the process?

Arin: I started at the beginning of my teaching career here, so both Rita and Angie brought me into the process. Angie was teaching at the junior level, Rita at the sophomore level, and I was at the senior level. For me it was really attractive because I wanted to work with experienced faculty, and I knew this project was longitudinal: I thought it was interesting that we would be doing something over a long period of time. I remember starting in the Lesson Study and being super excited about it, but having no idea of what it actually was. What reassured me was knowing that it had been done before: we have this big emphasis on evidence-based practice, and there was evidence that Lesson Study had been successful in other departments.

Angie: I decided to join it because I had been at conferences at the national level about evidence-based practice [EBP]. They talked about how nursing undergrads need exposure to EBP; this is the expectation to function in health care now. I looked at our curriculum, and it seemed like people were doing *some* of it, but it was really hodgepodge, random, all over the place. The concept of going across the whole curriculum really sold me on it; the idea that this could really change it for the whole curriculum and really change the way our students learn.

Arin: And there's the piece about information literacy. Coming from a clinical background, when you get in a clinical environment with new nurses, you want them to know how to look at some of those resources. This gave them very functional experience: we're doing something that matters, something they can apply right away when they graduate. We don't like to waste our time on things that aren't practical.

Rita: I would echo much of what they've said so far. I am thankful for CETL for seeking us out to participate in Lesson Study, and supporting/mentoring us throughout the project. I loved how the project was designed to be interdisciplinary. While we worked with librarians in the past, it was very superficial (in comparison to what it is now): we would tell them when we wanted them to come in, and they would do it, and that was about it. I knew Lesson Study could make our relationship deeper, better. And the topic area was really attractive to me: nursing programs are required to prepare students to demonstrate application of evidence-based practice, and this was an awesome, time-invested opportunity to scaffold training across our curriculum.

Describe your experience with library instruction before and after the Lesson Study.

Rita: When we first started talking, there were some differences. You know, "the nurses need this," or "this is how we do things," which [the librarians] were great and supportive of, but didn't fully understand: none of them had any first-hand experience . . . and none of them were married to nurses! We were truly blue and red. But it ended up being a great growing experience, and we came to understand each other on a much deeper level. Students recognized it too: without any prompting, they told us that it was obvious that [nursing and library staff] had a strong relationship.

Arin: I'll add to that: I teach research methods at the grad level, and I noticed that my students—even my graduate students—have a comfortable relationship with the librarians as a result of this project. My students aren't shy to ask them questions about assignments, and because the librarians have had experience with the nursing department, they are able to help them more completely. And on a personal level, I am more apt to ask for their help: before I would just try to figure out whatever it was by myself or go to one of my colleagues. But now that we've established a really approachable, friendly environment, I will deliberately seek out their expertise. I had a summer research assistant whom I set up with the librarians so she could get familiar with the resources. I never would have done that had I not had this working relationship with the librarians. And now other faculty are starting to do the same thing, which is really cool.

Angie: My usual approach was to e-mail the librarian and say, "Could you come on this day and talk about advanced database research?" or whatever topic I needed covered. I didn't know that they could tailor their presentation to my specific needs. Before—while they would always do what I asked—I'd think, "Oh, I wish they would've done this or that" after the presentation. I wouldn't even think to say, "This is the assignment I'm having my students work toward." Now I know they need to see the assignment so they can be more specific and prep better. And they are perfectly willing to do so, which is enormously helpful.

Arin: We have a better understanding now of each other's roles and expectations. It's easy to say, "Oh she/he's a nurse," but what does that really mean? By working closely with each other, we started to realize what our professions were actually like.

Rita: One librarian started using the nursing lingo after working with us for so long, and he actually knew what he was talking about!

What outcomes have you observed as a result of this collaboration?

Angie: I see outcomes from the student level, the faculty level, and my own personal level. Our students learned database skills that they can apply not only on our own campus but wherever they end up going. On a faculty level, we got comments across the department that students seem to know what they are doing more and more. And personally, Lesson Study has created a relationship with the librarians that you simply don't get outside of your department: I think it's safe to say we have closer relationships with the librarians than some people within our own department. Our relationship is more than just "hey, let's work together," it's actually quite meaningful.

Rita: We've really grown as three nursing faculty together, as well as with another discipline. It's been really powerful.

Arin: Teaching across all of the levels within the nursing program really makes the Lesson Study work. Since the librarians and nursing faculty introduce students to the concept of Lesson Study as sophomores, and the same format is used in junior and senior levels, it is evident that we value these skills and apparent that they are intentionally "threaded" through the curriculum. Now, as we embark on starting a new curriculum, the librarians are asking, "Where is the thread?" They recognize that this "threading of concepts" with reinforcement throughout the curriculum creates collaborative accountability. In other words, the instructors know what the students have been taught and are better prepared to build on this. Furthermore, the students learn more quickly, as they have the material presented in a recognized format, which allows for reinforcement throughout the levels. Because of this visible "threading" throughout the undergraduate program, I would estimate that undergraduate students are perhaps better prepared than the students entering graduate programs, where the curriculum is not as linear. Reinforcement makes learning stick much better than teaching something only one time.

Rita: At the end, my students were saying all of these wonderful comments like, "I've begun to enjoy research," or "I can critically think better." It was a moment where I was like, "could you repeat that again?" That was our goal! Hearing it expressed was the icing on the cake.

What was most challenging about this collaboration?

Arin: Our schedules could be tough to manage, though we really had no problem working around it: our group was very flexible and collaborative. And now I'm bringing it back to a positive.

Angie: In the beginning it was terminology. We had different names for different things. They brought in their standards for information literacy, and we brought in ours. In comparing, they were actually the same, but we just called them something different. Once we got over the language—through lots of negotiation—we were able to move forward.

Rita: There was a difference in priorities, too. We had some comical moments of "no, that doesn't happen in nursing" or "yes, that definitely happens in nursing!" But it always ended up being respectful and easy to work through.

Arin: Another thing was that we were busy and felt swamped sometimes. But when you are working on a project with passionate and motivated people, it's easy to feel energized and motivated yourself.

What was most valuable about this collaboration?

Arin: For me it's easy: the scaffolding of evidence-based practice throughout our curriculum. We are getting our students ready so that when they graduate, they can apply the skills they learned through this program right away.

Rita: And the reason that can happen was because we had both disciplines come to work. Students could get what they need from us and from the librarians. The collaboration *was* the most valuable thing to me.

Angie: We are teaching about evidence-based practice. And now we are *doing* a project that is modeling evidence-based practice for our students. We teach them about things like the interdisciplinary teams and quality improvement, and with this we have a real-life example to model for them.

Anything else you'd like to share about this experience that we didn't ask about?
Arin: At the end we all took a group picture, and it was cool to see the "face" of the group. I was sad to see it come to an end. It's easy to work on your own projects, but it's important for everyone to talk about what you are doing in your classes: we can do so much more if we have an awareness of what is going on in our department.
Angie: Now we have a new problem: we'll come to a meeting with library and we talk for half an hour to catch up with them.
Rita: Not a bad thing.

Bob Eierman, former director of the Center for Excellence in Teaching and Learning
Coordinated Lesson Study Revisions of Library One-Shots

Bob Eierman, professor of chemistry, earned a PhD in analytical chemistry and has been a UW–Eau Claire Chemistry Department faculty member since 1983. He has taught general chemistry, quantitative analysis, and instrumental analysis, and teaching methods courses for science education students. His scholarly work has focused on design, implementation, and assessment of college chemistry curriculum, particularly

Figure 10.4.   Bob Eierman. *UWEC Photography*

in quantitative analysis. He has studied creativity in teaching and the pedagogy of undergraduate research student mentoring and worked extensively with K–12 teachers to improve their science teaching through a series of federally funded summer workshops. He was the founding director of the UW–Eau Claire Center for Excellence in Teaching and Learning (CETL), a professional development support unit for educators that was created to promote excellent teaching and learning, and served in that position for five years.

During his time as the UW–Eau Claire's CETL director he learned about Lesson Study through Dr. Bill Cerbin from University of Wisconsin–La Crosse. Cerbin had been instrumental in bringing Lesson Study to college-level educators. He also became aware of the difficulties facing librarians in trying to teach information literacy in single 50-minute sessions within a disciplinary instructor's course. This led to creation of the first Lesson Study between the library and other disciplines' faculty.

How was working with the library Lesson Studies different from other Lesson Studies you conducted or observed?

The library Lesson Studies by necessity involved educators from two disciplines: the librarians and the academic discipline. In addition, the research lesson was taught by the librarian, who had no previous relationship with the students and limited relationship with the course curriculum. It was a single lesson of material that is related to, but different from, most of the course.

These [interdisciplinary Lesson Studies] differ from the typical Lesson Study in which participants are all from the same discipline and have extensive knowledge and experience teaching the lesson content. The result of these differences was that the discussions about the learning goals and the structure and details of the research lesson were longer and more complex because there was less common ground on the part of the different educators in building the lesson.

Traditionally Lesson Studies have been conducted in single disciplines. Why did you participate in three Lesson Studies with disciplinary and library faculty?

The type of lesson being taught was different than a typical disciplinary lesson. The content was not as familiar to the course instructors or well connected to most of the course content. Because the lesson instructor was not the day-to-day instructor, they were not familiar with the students or most of the content of the course. Bringing the librarians and content instructors together for extended discussions about the goals and structure of the research lesson was the vital component for success that has been missing in the past. These rich discussions revealed many challenges and misunderstandings that had reduced the effectiveness of previous lessons and helped the instructors get on the same page.

Another critical aspect of the library Lesson Studies was that there was a carefully crafted and systematic approach taken to assessing the depth and breadth of student learning in the lesson. The participants who were not teaching observed the lesson and gathered important information about how the lesson was received and what the students learned. For many, this was the first time they had engaged in an observation exercise like this, and it is typically a very enlightening experience. Participants also analyzed student papers produced during the lesson to assess their learning, and in some cases they held student focus-group discussions to get feedback on the student experience. The combination of types of student feedback made it possible to recognize what was effective and what was not, which allowed changes to improve subsequent offerings of the lesson.

The meeting of educators from different disciplines was challenging, but it also created an amazing amount of exciting and fascinating discussion and progress. The participants were eager to make things work, and it was a great pleasure to observe them working together toward the common goal of an effective lesson.

What were the challenges you faced in your role in the Lesson Study?

My role was to keep the Lesson Study process on track as educators from two different academic worlds came together to create an effective lesson. There were frequently times when disciplinary language and pedagogies had to be sorted out. Educators were excited to work across disciplinary boundaries, but compromise was necessary to build a coherent whole. The Lesson Study process is important to achieving a positive outcome, and I was able to serve as the guide to slow things down or speed them up so we kept on track and got things done in a timely manner.

Setting learning goals was challenging because of the varying expertise of the librarians and disciplinary educators. The underlying knowledge and skill base required significant discussion to become clear and to set some limits on how much could be addressed in a single lesson. Next we moved to the lesson design, and that also required much brainstorming, discussion, and compromise. Finally, we spent a significant amount of effort creating an assessment structure that would provide the feedback we needed to recognize success. We met for an hour a week, and the time slipped by quickly so we had to make good use of the face-to-face time and set reasonable tasks to be completed between sessions. I would frequently sit quiet during the discussions but had to recognize when it was time to move on or to work a bit more on the task at hand.

Any challenges I had were made easier by the excellent professionals who worked on these Lesson Studies. They worked hard but were open and creative throughout the process. Many strong relationships have resulted in addition to the excellent lessons.

Why Lesson Study and not something else?

The Lesson Study [LS] process—design, implement, and assess a single lesson in a group—is exactly what was needed to create effective library lessons. The LS structure requires a long-term commitment to succeed in creating a single lesson. We were able to engage educators in extensive discussion about a lesson that they deeply care about. The process is actually a best practice in creating excellent lessons, but we rarely are able to take the time to work so extensively on a single lesson. The amount and types of student feedback that we received was also critical in optimizing the impact of the lesson in subsequent courses. Finally, I think most participants experienced a full-blown cycle of lesson creation that helped them recognize what it takes to create excellent student learning.

What advice would you give other librarians interested in undertaking Lesson Study on their campuses?

Lesson Study takes a large commitment of time and effort to be successful. This needs to come from both the library staff and the academic educators. The culture of both the library and the disciplinary department must be supportive of this type of work because it will pull people away from other efforts. I think that being sure people recognize the level of effort, but also the potential gains from this sort of effort, must happen before it starts in order to enable ultimate success.

In order for the curricular changes to be made, the participants must have their department's support and willingness to change. Lesson Study can lead to big, valuable changes, but only if the cultures of the departments support that change.

Information literacy is a critical component of a college education, and I believe this Lesson Study structure is an excellent way to overcome many of the barriers to creating effective learning experiences for students. We recognized that educators and students alike underestimate the complexity and difficulty of helping students learn to use the sophisticated and powerful tools that exist in academia and the world today.

Conclusion

We have looked at the genesis of information literacy instruction and the persistent one-shot. The one-shot instruction session has evolved over decades, driven by and responding to changes in technology, pedagogy, and learning styles. It has had its detractors, librarians chief among them, frustrated that it is an inadequate model for teaching information literacy. And yet it has endured. There is something about the model that works, and rather than lamenting its shortcomings, it is more productive for librarians to actively embrace its possibilities. Throughout this book we have discussed strategies for doing so. Too often we conflate the idea of a one-shot lesson with a stand-alone lesson. The former is not, and should not be, the latter. On the contrary, the one-shot lesson, when conceived of as a careful and intentional collaboration between librarians and teaching faculty and fully integrated into the curriculum, can be the foundation of a robust multifaceted information literacy program. As we have said in this book, a one-shot library session is not the only shot a student gets at information literacy. With planning and intentionality, one-shots can be scaffolded throughout a curriculum so that one shot builds on another as students work their way through a program or major. Additionally, the process of planning the one-shot can be the impetus that brings librarians and disciplinary faculty together, and can result in collaborations that transcend the single 50-minute session.

As we conclude this book, which is a reflection of our experience, research, and experimentation thus far, we want to emphasize that our work with the one-shot is not complete. It never will be. As long as information, students, higher education, technology, pedagogy, and the world keep changing, the one-shot must keep evolving as well. Even at this writing the Association of College & Research Libraries (ACRL) is in the process of developing and revising a *Framework for Information Literacy for Higher Education*,[1] a new document guiding librarians in the understanding and teaching of information literacy.

In this book, we have talked about identifying and working within existing structures. In order to do so, it is imperative that librarians keep abreast of what those structures are, the challenges to those existing structures, and the changes underway and anticipated. This means constantly assessing the existing arrangement, not only of the library and the institution but of the culture, society, and economies in which these structures exist. At this writing, higher education—especially the public institution—is facing increased scrutiny from legislators looking for increased accountability coupled with decreased funding. At the same time, institutions of higher education are looking at changing demographics, which means a decrease in traditionally aged and prepared students and an increase in competition to attract and retain those students. What do these issues have to do with the library and, in particular, the library one-shot lesson? Those are exactly the questions librarians need to be asking themselves. They need to be making those connections and articulating them clearly for decision makers and power brokers. Our campus is currently looking at strategies for improving that important measure of time toward graduation. How can we ensure that more students will graduate in four years? On the surface, it may seem like this is an issue that does not involve the library. However, the one-shot can be part of the solution. How, you ask? By not requiring—or even advocating for—a stand-alone information literacy credit, even though we heartily value information literacy, we are offering a solution that does not increase the number of requirements that students must meet to graduate. Instead, we are putting efforts into embedding this skill into the existing classes that students already take.

The library one-shot is a model in which the institution takes responsibility for embedding and integrating a desired outcome into the curriculum. Rather than placing the onus on the student to fit in yet another separate, costly requirement that has the potential to extend the time to graduation, the institution is ensuring that intended content is built into the education that students receive. Think of it as iodized salt, where a necessary component (iodine) is integrated into the content so successfully and seamlessly that they are no longer thought of as separate entities. We need not only to do this, but we need to let people on campus know that we are intentionally doing this. It is a connection no one else on campus is likely to make if librarians don't articulate it for them. It is also a model that can serve as an example for embedding and integrating other requirements that extend a student's stay on campus and that require human and capital resources at levels that are no longer sustainable. Again, no one outside the library is likely to see the connection unless librarians actively make it.

In addition to making and communicating connection between what we do and larger forces, librarians should also be making connections between the values and standards defined in our own profession and those of other professions. Simply stated, we need to practice framing our issues in terms that resonate with external audiences. The aforementioned ACRL *Framework* provides a tool to help us do this. Reflecting the direction taken by educators in other disciplines, the new *Framework* emphasizes "threshold concepts" over discrete skills. Threshold concepts are defined as those core concepts that are fundamental to understanding and acquiring expertise in a given field of knowledge. They are more complex to learn, teach, and assess than an inventory of concrete skills. The idea of threshold concepts is used across disciplines in higher education, so it is likely to be familiar to the faculty with whom we collaborate. Additionally, the threshold concepts themselves align with those used in other disciplines. For example, the emphases of the ACRL *Framework* on critical thinking and rhetorical knowledge are very much aligned with the *Framework for Success in Postsecondary Writing*, developed by the Council of Writing Program Administrators, the National Council of Teachers of English, and the National Writing Project.[2] A 2013 report looked at commonalities among various outcomes frameworks in higher education. It identified seven key domains, most if not all of which are represented in the ACRL *Framework* and overlap with components of information literacy that librarians have long embraced. They include creativity ("the generation of new ideas" or "novel integration of existing ideas"), critical thinking, teamwork, effective communication, digital and information literacy, citizenship, and life skills. [3] Librarians must embrace the idea, as the drafters of the ACRL *Framework* have, that the outcomes for which we aim do not exist parallel to and separate from those of other disciplines and areas of knowledge. Rather they are essential components of learning across disciplines, and the way we teach them should be fully integrated and embedded and inseparable. The commonalities among our respective guiding documents can be invoked to encourage collaboration.

Throughout, the *Framework* document advocates and recognizes the need for collaboration between librarians and teaching faculty. The importance of collaboration in information literacy is underscored by the inclusion of nonlibrarian faculty and administrators on the task force that developed the *Framework*, as well as by a section of the narrative aimed specifically at faculty and administrators. The *Framework* provides sample assignments for librarians and faculty as inspiration for teaching these concepts. The *Framework* acknowledges the ubiquity of the one-shot in library instruction and the importance of collaboration so that it becomes the building block of a comprehensive information literacy program:

> Over the course of a student's academic program, one-shot sessions that address a particular need at a particular time, systematically integrated into the curriculum, can play a significant role in an information literacy program. It is important for librarians and teaching faculty to understand that the *Framework* is not designed to be implemented in a single information literacy session in a student's academic career; it is intended to be developmentally and systematically integrated into the student's academic program at a variety of levels.[4]

Who would have predicted that the one-shot model would endure? The authors of this book have been involved in library instruction collectively for decades, beginning when we were still talking about bibliographic instruction. Various models have come and gone and come again, trends have passed, predictions have been made, and through it all the one-shot model has remained a prevalent one. Looking ahead, few can predict with certainty what the future has in store for higher education, libraries, and library instruction. But librarians will do what they have always done: pay attention, experiment, and adapt. At this writing, institutions of higher education are struggling with budget issues and diminishing numbers in the traditional demographic of college students. At the same time students are coming to us with changing and ever-increasing access and expectations to information and technology. The nature of information itself never stops changing. A few years ago we were not talking about how or when to cite a tweet. What does attribution mean in something like Storify or a blog when you are embedding or linking to that source, and how does it differ from a traditional research paper written in APA or MLA style? How does the open access movement, proliferation of new media and genres for publication, questionable practices in scholarly publishing,[5] or corporate sponsorship of research call into question the conventions we have been using to identify credible sources of information? How do changes in the ownership, control, and regulation of news and information outlets challenge our notions about information? All of this is to say that librarians must remain ever vigilant so that the one-shot does not become a static, stale vestige of a bygone era, but rather a constantly evolving integrated component of higher education.

NOTES

1. "Framework for Information Literacy for Higher Education," Association of College & Research Libraries, http://acrl.ala.org/ilstandards/.

2. Council of Writing Program Administrators, National Council of Teachers of English, and National Writing Project, "Framework for Success in Postsecondary Writing" (white paper, Council of Writing Program Administrators, National Council of Teachers of English, National Writing Project, January 2011), http://wpacouncil.org/files/framework-for-success -postsecondary-writing.pdf.

3. Markle, Ross, et al. "Synthesizing Frameworks of Higher Education Student Learning Outcomes" (research report, Educational Testing Service, November 2013), http://www.ets .org/Media/Research/pdf/RR-13-22.pdf.

4. "Framework for Information Literacy for Higher Education Draft 2" (working paper, Association of College & Research Libraries, June 2014), lines 128–135, http://acrl.ala.org/ ilstandards/wp-content/uploads/2014/11/Framework-for-IL-for-HE-draft-3.pdf.

5. John Bohannon, "Who's Afraid of Peer Review?" *Science* 342, no. 6154 (2013): 60–65. doi:10.1126/science.342.6154.60.

Appendix A

First-Year Composition
Lesson Study Outline v. 1

(5 min.) Welcome to the library

In this session we will explore some research tools. We'll start with a quick demonstration of searching the library catalog and a library database for journal articles, and then you will begin working on your topics with the help of a partner. At the end we will come back together to discuss our research experiences. There are more research tools and strategies available to you than we will be able to cover today, so please remember one of the most important library resources available to you: people. Library staff are here to help you when you have questions during your research process. You can stop by the reference desk; reach us by phone, chat, e-mail; or set up an appointment with a librarian.

(5 min.) Catalog search

My research topic looks at the phenomenon of bullying on the Internet.
Catalog (from home page):

- Expect to find books, videos, other media, government documents, *not* journal articles.
- Enter: bullying Internet (note that it's not a question or phrase, just content-bearing words).
- The first three results mention cyberbullying, but are not consistent in how the term is written.
- Click on the first result to illustrate subject headings (standardized spelling of *cyberbullying*, broader terms), mention location information and call number.

(5–10 min.) Database search

Use databases to find journal articles, newspaper articles, magazine articles—usually more current information than books.

- Databases by topic: have students choose a topic (discipline) likely to include information on cyberbullying
- Multidisciplinary databases vs. specialized databases
- From list of recommended databases, select Academic Search Complete
- Enter: cyberbullying
- Discuss results:
  - Click on record for abstract and headings
  - Fulltext vs. Find It
  - Methods for limiting search results (e.g., scholarly only or add search term like "middle school")

(15–20 min.) Exercise (handout outlining steps)

- **(2 min.)** Intro to activity: "Now you get to work on your search topics. [*Assign partners. Distribute worksheet*].
- Put your name on the sheet and exchange worksheets with your partner. Now that you have your partner's sheet, put your name down for 'searcher.' First, one of you will each describe your topic to your partner. You will have about 2 minutes to do this, then I will ask you to switch and the other person in your pair will describe his/her topic. Write down your partner's research topic. As you listen to your partner, jot down words, phrases and ideas that you hear, as well as any synonyms or related ideas that come to you. Ask clarifying questions if you need to, as you will be doing a search on your partner's topic."
- **(2 min.)** First partner describes topic. Call the switch.
- **(2 min.)** Second partner describes topic.
- **(7 min.)** Search on partner's topic. Write down steps and results.
- **(3 min.)** Partners share results
  - Can you tell what the information source is?
  - Does it look like it will be useful?
  - Do you have enough information to find it?

(10 min.) Entire group comes together to discuss results

- Librarian asks focused questions such as:
  - Whose partner came up with what looks like the perfect source for your topic?
  - Did anyone have trouble finding anything for their partner?
  - Did anyone search the library catalog and come up with nothing on their topic?
  - What challenges did you face in searching for a journal article?
- Librarian comments on observations.

Wrap up

Appendix B

Lesson Study Observation Guidelines

SPATIAL CONCERNS

Seating chart: Shevaun should quickly note where/how her students are arranged around the room once everyone is settled.

Observers should take note of the general area/row of their own observations, including the gender and race of the students in their areas, any vacant spots, clutter at each work station, etc.

ENGAGEMENT DURING THE LESSON

Are the students engaged? Nodding their heads? Taking notes? Laughing at jokes by instructor or responding to questions? Interested in the topic and information as indicated by facial expression and body language (leaning forward? Looking at Jill as she's speaking?)

Conversely, do the students seem confused or disinterested? Are they looking around trying to see what their neighbors are doing? Are they raising their hands or considering it? Are they texting, Facebooking, whispering, doing homework for another class, or otherwise being distracted? Are they slumping, dozing, or staring fixedly into the distance?

Are students following along on computers? If so, are they able to keep up? Do they get lost? Are they looking over their peers' shoulders for clarification? Do they get sidetracked and begin searching for their own topics or goofing off?

If not following along, why? Are they intently listening and watching the big screen? Did they attempt to follow along and then give up? Are they note-taking instead?

PEER ACTIVITY

Do the students actively participate? Do they dive right in and begin talking/sharing, or is there a lull or confusion? Are they using the worksheet? Are they following the prompts that were given orally and noted on the worksheet? Approximately how many terms/phrases do they note? Do any hands go into the air for assistance or with questions? Is there enough time for both students to share their topics or does one get short shrift?

When they move to the database search, do they do so with conviction and purpose? Do they know where to go, or is there discussion or confusion? Do the partners work together or independently? Are the students using the notes and key phrases they took down from their partners or just searching from memory? Are they consulting the prompts on the worksheets or each other? Are they asking for assistance from Jill or Shevaun?

RESULTS OF SEARCHING

From what you can observe, were the students able to turn up reasonable sources (limitwise, in appropriate databases)? Did they stop at their first find or seem to actually evaluate their results?

Appendix C

First-Year Composition
Lesson Study Worksheet v. 1

ENG 110—Library Research

Name_____

Name of your partner_____

1. As your partner describes his/her research topic, jot down some of the words and ideas you hear.

Research topic:

Keywords:

2. Now you can begin looking for one *really good* source for your partner's research. It is up to you to determine whether the source is a book, journal article, etc.
Where did you search?

Record the steps you took to find the source:

3. List the source you found. Record enough information so that your partner can find it again.

Appendix D

First-Year Composition Lesson Study Outline v. 2

(2 min.) Welcome to the library

- Distribute exercise sheet.

(20 min.) Catalog search

- **(3 min.) Demonstration**
- **(12 min. total) Exercise 1**
  - ° **(4 min.)** Pairs share their topics and ask any clarifying questions, taking notes.
  - ° **(2 min.)** Brainstorm keywords for partner's topic.
  - ° Instructions to search for partner's topic.
  - ° **(4 min.)** Search in the catalog for a book or other source on their topic. On the exercise sheet, write down the information about one promising result.
  - ° **(2 min.)** Share your result with your partner. Discuss how you found the item.
- **(5 min.) Discussion**
  - ° Whose partner came up with what looks like *the* perfect source for your topic?
  - ° Did anyone have trouble finding anything for their partner?
  - ° What strategies did you use? (search strategies on handout)
  - ° Discuss strategies for moving from one good result to another (subject headings, call numbers). Broadening a topic.

(20 min.) Database search

- **(3 min.) Demonstration**
- **(10 min. total) Exercise 2**
  - ° **(4 min.)** Now you will work with your partner to search on your topics. Identify which partner will do the searching first. Direct students to Academic Source Complete.

° **(4 min.)** Switch so that the second partner now does the searching. Partners work together to find an article on the second topic.
° **(2 min.)** Now you get to work on your search topics together. Work with your partner to find an article on your topic. Then switch to find an article on your partner's topic.
- **(7 min.) Discuss**
  Librarian asks focused questions such as the following:
  ° Whose partner came up with what looks like *the* perfect source for your topic?
  ° Did anyone have trouble finding anything for their partner?
  ° What challenges did you face in searching for a journal article?
  ° How can one good source lead you to others?
  ° Did you have trouble getting the actual article?

(5 min.) Wrap up

Appendix E

First-Year Composition
Lesson Study Worksheet v. 2

ENG 110— Library Research

Name_____

Name of your partner_____

1. As your partner describes his/her research topic, **take notes**.

2. What are some **related words** that you could also use (e.g., "teens" or "teenagers," "movie" or "film")?

3. Working independently, **search in the library catalog** for one *really good* source **for your partner's research**. Write down enough information so that your partner can find it again:

4. Working with your partner, **search in Academic Search Complete** for one *really good* article **for your research** topic. Write down enough information so that you can find it again:

Not finding anything? Try these strategies to modify your search by

- broadening
- narrowing
- parallel concept
- time
- geography

Example: Cyberbullying

- Broadening: Bullying
- Narrowing: Prosecution of cyberbullies
- Parallel: Stalking
- Time: Cyberbullying pre-SMS (texting)
- Geography: Cyberbullying and China's growing data network

Example: Southern Plantations

- Broadening: Estate farm
- Narrowing: Slave-holding plantations
- Parallel: South American coffee plantations
- Time: 18th-century Southern plantation
- Geography: Charleston, S.C., area

Appendix F

First-Year Composition
Lesson Study Outline v. 3

(3 min.) Welcome to the library

In this session we will explore some research tools for finding books, journal articles, and other media that are necessary and appropriate for doing college-level research. You will be working with a partner because (1) your partner can bring a different perspective to the topic, and (2) it gives you the opportunity to step back from your own topic for a moment and focus on search strategies.
Distribute activity sheet.

(5–8 min.) Topic discussion pair and share

First you will each describe your topic to your partner. You will have about two minutes to do this, then I will ask you to switch, and the other person in your pair will describe his/her topic. As you listen to your partner, jot down words, phrases and ideas that you hear as well as any synonyms or related ideas that come to you. Ask clarifying questions if you need to, as you will be doing a search on your partner's topic.

(30–40 min.) Library Search

- **(1 min.) Introduce Library Search**
  - ° This tool searches for articles, books, media, and more.

- **(5–10 min.) Partner search**
  - ° Search for a really good source on your partner's topic. *[During this time the librarian should be moving around the room answering questions, observing, and gathering examples for discussion.]*

- **(10 min.) Discussion**
  - ° Whose partner came up with what looks like *the* perfect source for your topic?
  - ° What makes it a really good source?
  - ° What did you discover in choosing search terms that worked well or didn't work well?
  - ° Did anyone have trouble finding anything for their partner? Why might it be a good thing if you didn't find the perfect source?
  - ° Look at the results. Do you see mostly one kind of resource or a wide variety? Why might that be?
  - ° What strategies did people use (facets? Different words?)
  - ° Thinking back on the information cycle, do most of your results come from similar points along the cycle or are they representative of several points? How might you revise your search to bring in a wider range of sources.

- **(5–10 min.) Your own search**
  - ° This time search on your own topic. Using strategies from the discussion, try to find a resource that represents a different point on the information cycle from that found by your partner.

- **(10 min.) Discussion**
  - ° Who found something different but good? What strategies did you use?
  - ° In looking at the results from your search, can you determine various disciplines that might have an interest in your topic? [*Possibly mention databases by discipline as a more advanced avenue for searching.*]
  - ° What are strategies for saving good results?

(5 min.) Wrap up
There are many more research tools and strategies available that will be valuable for this research assignment as well as future ones. Library staff are here to help you when you have questions during your research process. You can stop by the reference desk, reach us by phone, chat, or e-mail, or set up an appointment with a librarian.

Appendix G

First-Year Composition
Lesson Study Worksheet v. 3

ENG 110—Library Research

Your name_____

Name of your partner_____; E-mail address_____

1. As your partner describes his/her research topic, **take notes**. What are some **related words** that you could also use (e.g., "teens" or "teenagers," "movie" or "film")?

2. Use Library Search to find a source for your partner's research. Can you find an item that looks like it could be useful for your partner?

Discuss results with your partner, and if he/she finds them useful, e-mail results to your partner. Give the sheet to your partner.

3. Now turn your attention to your own research topic. Try searching for sources on your own topic.

Appendix H

Lesson Study in the Sciences Preclass Worksheet and Handouts

Appendix 8

Accessing the Chemistry Literature Pre-Lab Assignment

☑ Meet with your advisor and come up with a question or two, related to your research project, that you wish to research in the literature.

Your question(s):

☑ Create a list of keywords that will help you find the relavant references

Your keywords:

☑ Look over the "A Guide to the Accessing the Chemistry Literature" (see attached)

☑ Create and EndNotesWeb account. (see attached)

A Guide to Accessing the Chemistry Literature

The Literature:

Chemistry Literature is the published body of knowledge, or knowledge-base, that forms the foundation of chemistry research. This literature comes in a variety of forms. Below are the more important forms, arranged from the more general to the more specific in terms of content.

- Textbooks: Used to convey well established ideas and concepts within a given field. For most students of chemistry, textbooks represent their first encounter with the knowledge base of chemistry.

- Topical Books: These give an overview of work in a more narrowly defined field that is also well established. These books have titles such as The Hydrogen Bond or Freidel-Crafts and Related Reactions.

- Monographs and Series: Like topical books, these are also a detailed written study of a sinagle specialized subject or an aspect of it. Often they come in a form of an arranged collection of related review articles on a specific topic. These have titles such as Advances in Protein Chemistry or Annual Review of Biochemistry.

- Review Articles: These are articles published in a journal format and summarize the recent literature about a given topic. Some journals publish review articles along with primary research articles, while others focus exclusively on review articles. Examples in the chemistry literature include the journal Chemical Reviews, which publishes current summaries of work in a given area, and Accounts of Chemical Research, which publishes review articles summarizing the work of a particular researcher or a small group of collaborators. Review articles are a very good way to get up to speed on what is known about a research topic you may be interested in studying.

- Primary Research Articles: These represent the core of all chemistry literature and report on the findings of original research. Usually these finding have never been published before and therefore represent a new chunk of knowledge that is being added to the growing knowledge-base of chemistry. These articles can come in different forms, such as a Communications, which typically are quite short (2 pages or less) and report on a late-breaking finding, or as Full Length Articles, which present a more in-depth and detailed report on a finding.

Journals:

The journals that publish both review and primary research articles can be categorized based on their target audiences:

- Broad, general interest science journals: These contain very significant, high impact articles written for a general science audience (e.g. Nature, Science, Proceedings of the National Academy of Sciences). They contain not only chemistry-related articles, but also articles from other disciplines. There is a good deal of prestige attached to publishing in these journals, where your findings are more likely to get picked up by the mainstream media.

- Journals spanning the entire discipline of chemistry: These also contain very significant articles and written for chemists from all subfields (e.g. Journal of the American Chemical Society (JACS), Angewandte Chemie International Edition, Chemical Communications, etc.).

- Journals that span a given sub-field: Articles that are significant to chemists across a given subfield, but not entirely specialized (e.g. Inorganic Chemistry, Journal of Physical Chemistry, Biochemistry, Journal of Organic Chemistry, etc.).

- Journals serving specific specialties within a subfield. Very specialized to specific research areas. (e.g. Journal of Molecular Spectroscopy, Journal of Inorganic Biochemistry, Liquid Crystals, Journal of Computational Chemistry, etc.).

Literature Databases:

One of the best ways of searching for what you what you are looking for in the literature is to use literature databases. The records in these databases are references to the literature. Each reference contains a number of of fields that describe the reference, such Author, Title, Journal of Publication, Year Published, Type of Article, etc. The databases also contain tools for searching these fields to find the records you are interested in. These databases can now be searched over the Internet using a web browser. Like journals, different databases are targeted to different audiences. Below are the databases available to us at UW-Eau Claire, which can be used to find references in the chemistry literature.

- **Web of Science** (Part of the Web of Knowledge)
  - Broad focus across disciplines.
  - Free access from on campus (Go through the McIntyre Library Website).
  - You can create an optional login that will allow you to save your searches.
  - Limited to references published from 1987 to present.
  - Can do cited reference searches, where you can search for all the references that have cited a particular reference.
  - Can easily save reference to the EndNoteWeb reference manager.

- **PubMed** (U. S. National Library of Medicine, NIH)
  - Broad focus around biomedical related disciplines, including chemistry.
  - Free access from anywhere (http://www.ncbi.nlm.nih.gov/sites/entrez).
  - Can search for a specific reference.

- **SciFinder** (Chemical Abstracts)
  - More narrow but very in-depth focus on the chemistry literature.
  - Free access from on campus, but must first create a login (Go through the McIntyre Library Website)
  - A very limited number of people (5) can be accessing the database at the same time.
  - Has some very powerful search tools, for example, you can search on a reaction, a molecule, or just a part of a molecule, by using a web-based tool to draw it on screen.

Notes:
- How significant is a given article?

  A simple, though often misleading rule for overall significance of a given article is that the more general the audience of the journal, the more significant or "high impact" the finding is. However, a more valid metric of "impact" is the number of times a work has been cited by others in the literature, and sometimes a paper attracts more readers when it is published in a more specialized journal, because that is where members of that particular research community will most likely look for articles that they are interested in reading. In this workshop you will learn how to carry out a Cited Reference Search, which allows you to find who has cited a particular article.

- So, what type of article should I look for?

  It depends on your need. All of the types of sources listed above have their merits.

  - To write a paper in a lower-level class, you may not need to get any more specific than what you might find at the monograph level.

  - If you are writing a paper for an upper-level class you may want to look for review articles that focus on your topic. You may may also want to bring your discussion up-to-date by including recent primary research articles as well.

  - If you are writing for research purposes, be it a proposal or a journal article, it is key to review all of the current articles related to your work. Active scholars need to keep as up-to-date with the literature as they can (this can be daunting!), because they need to be aware of how new developments may affect the context of their work. Also, new developments can spark new ideas. In this workshop you will learn about a tool called EndNotes, which can help you with managing this task.

- So how do I get started on building a bibliography?

  - Review articles are a good way to start building your bibliography. Review articles give you a good broad overview and usually have an extensive list of references that can help get you started.

  - Once you have found some key, ground-breaking articles in your area of interest, use them to do a cited reference search to find out who is currently publishing findings in your area of interest, as indicated by their interest in these same key, ground-breaking articles.

--EndNote Web Workshop--

EndNote Web (ENW) is a web-based research and writing tool designed to help students and researchers through the process of writing a research paper. You can organize your references for citing in papers, it also can be used as the perfect complement to EndNote and other desktop writing tools.

EndNote Web is free for all at the University of Wisconsin-Eau Claire because the Library has a subscription to Thompson ISI Web of Knowledge.

EndNote Web lets you:

-Import references from hundreds of online bibliographic databases and organize a library of references
-Store up to 10,000 records
-Share EndNote Web groups and view groups shared by others
-Use over 3,200 publishing styles to format in-text citations and bibliographies
-Cite While You Write™ in Microsoft Word (requires plug-in) to insert references and format papers instantly
-Format papers in other word processors using RTF (rich text format) files
-ISI Web of Knowledge, EndNote, and EndNote Web are designed to work seamlessly together and streamline your research:
-EndNote Web transfers references directly to EndNote on the desktop

Need Help –

Here is the link to the "How To" page from the Course and Research Guides there are tutorials help files located here http://libguides.uwec.edu/endnote

I am always willing to try and help out in any way I can.
Hans Kishel
kishelhf@uwec.edu
715-836-2959
1001A McIntyre Library

Create an account or log in:
Navigate to the web site MyEndNoteWeb.com
Then register as a new user or log in to you ISI Web of Knowledge account

A brief tour of EndNote Web:

Opening Screen
Help: The help system for ENW is actually very helpful
Main Tabs –
My References – This is where we are right now, Collect, Organize, Format, Options
My References –
Shows all of you references
Shows all of your folders/groups
Getting Start Guide – These tutorials walk you through some of the basics for getting started
Collect Tab –
Online Search – You can connect to databases or library catalogs directly through ENW. I do not recommend using this feature. You will have more control over your searches in the databases themselves from the library web page.
New Reference – Add a reference by hand
Import References – This allows you to import saved references to your ENW Library. If you customize the list of filters you will only see the filters you have added to your favorites list.
Organize Tab –
Manage My Groups –

1

New Group button - Allows you to create a new group/folder
Share/Manage Sharing – Add email addresses of people you wish to give access to your references
Other's Groups – To see the groups that others have added you too

Format Tab –

Bibliography – Choose a group of references to format into a bibliography which you can save, view, print, or email
Cite While You Write Plug-In – Allows you to add a web plug in to insert references from your ENW while you write papers in MS Word
Format Paper – Allows you to take Rich Text Format papers you have prepared and format them with your references in ENW *More on this later*
Export References – Choose a folder or group and then choose what format you want to export the references in

Options Tab –

Download Installers – "Cite While you Write" and Firefox extensions

Import References:

From Web of Knowledge (Science/Science Citation Index) there is a button [Save to **EndNote Web**] that will allow you to import the citation that you are looking at automatically.

From almost all EBSCO databases you can import a citation with just a couple of mouse clicks.

In the detailed record view you start by clicking on [icon] in the top right corner. Then choose the option for "Direct Export to EndNote Web"

For other databases as well as the above two, I have created tutorials that will walk you through the process for importing citations to your EndNote Web.
These can be found at:

http://libguides.uwec.edu/endnote

By choosing the "How to Import Citations" tab, and then clicking on the database provider you wish to see how to use.

Format a Paper

Now with the records that you have collected you can format a paper.

Then in your ENW:

Choose: **Format Tab**
Format Paper
   File – Browse to the location of the saved paper. The file must be saved as a **Rich Text Format (*.rtf file)**
Bibliographic Style
   You have a large number of styles to choose from.

Show **format paper preferences** to see how you need to write the paper to indicate that EndNote should insert a reference.
   By default the {} brackets are used to indicate that there is citation information.
Then Format
   A new rtf file is created and you can name and save it to where you like, but don't save over the original file so that if there are problems you can edit the original.

Appendix I

Lesson Study in the Sciences
In-Class Worksheet

The Research Process - An Exercise

The research process that you use today parallels the scientific research process that you should already be familiar with.

At the conclusion of this exercise you should have a basic understanding of some of the library's resources for conducting research.

Log into your EndNote Web account

Selecting a database
What is a database? - A database is a collection of information (in this case references to scientific literature) that has been organized so that it can be searched easily.

Conducting the Search

Looking at your topic, keywords, and the database you will be searching, write a search strategy to use to find information on your topic.

Example of search strategy

Topic? Groundwater Lake interaction at the near shore

Keywords?
        Groundwater   Ground water
        near shore   shore
        seepage   surface water interaction

Search
        Groundwater (in Topic)
   AND
        Seepage (in Topic)
   AND
        Surface water interaction (in Topic)

Tips / Things to Remember

Library Home Page - uwec.edu/Library/

myendnoteweb.com

Databases by Topic

Click on the "i" to get information
  on the database

Select best database for your research or
  select one of the multi-discipline databases

Searching and Refining

What is your question or topic?

Record your Keywords

Hint: You need to document this clearly enough so that someone else could replicate your search and get the same results. Just like you would need to in the methodology section of research paper.

Your work needs to be reproducable.

Example of Refine in writing

Initial Search Strategy	# of Results	Useful references? (Yes/No)
Groundwater (in Topic) AND Seepage (in Topic) AND Surface water interaction (in Topic)	74	Yes

Refined Search Strategy (eg. Removed keyword)	# of Results	Useful references? (Yes/No)
(Add / Remove Keywords) Groundwater (in Topic) AND Seepage (in Topic)	1280	Yes

Hint: At the top of screen after **"Results"** is a list of what you searched.
Which is part of your search strategy.

Tips / Things to Remember

How many text boxes can you use to write your search

How are those text boxes connected

What is each text box searching in

Adjust your keywords based on the way that the database refers to the topic

Read the abstract of a related reference for keywords that you may not have used

Are the references peer-reviewed

Related references based on shared

Search/Refine Table

The first four refine boxes indicate how you should refine your search.

Initial Search Strategy	# of Results	Useful references? (Yes/No)

Refined Search Strategy (eg. Removed keyword)	# of Results	Useful references? (Yes/No)
(Add / Remove Keywords)		
(Add / Remove Subject Areas)		
(Choose Article Type)		
(Sort by times Cited)		

Tips / Things to Remember

Strategies to Narrow your search:
  Add keywords
  Fewer Years
  Fewer Subject areas
  One or two reference types
  Select one or a few Source titles

Strategies to Widen your search:
  Remove keywords
  More Years
  All Subject areas
  All Article types
  All Source titles

Finding subject areas

Finding author-supplied keywords

Looking at the references for a paper that is closer to your topic

Use the Search History

Selecting an Article

Record two references that look like they will be useful in answering or addressing your research question/topic. Write a few sentences for each reference you chose to justify why you selected it related to your research question/topic.

Save the references to your EndNote Web, and create a group/folder so that you can start gathering information on this research topic.

Access the reference(s) you selected, to find the location of the articles/items?

Reproduce the Search - Exchange your exercise with someone else

Using all the information in the Search/Refine Table perform the same search/refine as the original searcher.

Name of Reviewer:

Did the number of results match at each step of the process?

Were you able to find the same articles that were found and recorded as being useful?

Tips / Things to Remember
Title
Type of reference (Review article)
Number of Citations
Abstract
Scholarly (peer-reviewed) articles
Source (Journal)
Year of publication
Author
Language
Pages

Log into your account: myendnoteweb.com
You can then save all the references you
    discover for your research

"Find It" - Button searches all ways that
    the reference is available through
    the library

Appendix J

Lesson Study in Nursing Prerequisite Worksheet

Nursing 240 Exercise – Types of Literature

Directions: Using the packet of articles, determine the category in which each article fits by placing a Y or N in the appropriate box and write a sentence about your rationale for why you placed them in a given category.

Example:

Weight loss, exercise, or both and physical function in obese older adults. 🔎

Villareal DT; Chode S; Parimi N; Sinacore DR; Hilton T; Armamento-Villareal R; Napoli N; Qualls C; Shah K; **New England Journal of Medicine**, 2011 Mar 31; 364 (13): 1218-29 (journal article - randomized controlled trial, research) ISSN: 0028-4793 PMID: 21449785

Subjects: Activities of Daily Living; Diet, Reducing; Exercise Physiology; Frail Elderly; Obesity; Weight Loss; Aged: 65+ years; Female; Male

Database: CINAHL Plus with Full Text

Article #	Scholarly Source	Popular Source	Trade Source	Primary Source	Secondary Source	Peer Reviewed	What characteristics led you to putting it into a specific category?
Example	Y	N	N	Y	N	Y	*It's scholarly because the NEJM is a scholarly/peer reviewed journal. It's a primary source because it has original research done through a randomized controlled trial.*
1							
2							
3							
4							
5							

Appendix K

Lesson Study in Nursing—
Sophomore Worksheet

Research - Finding information for your PICO question

At the conclusion of this exercise you should have a basic understanding of some of the library's resources for conducting research.

Introduction to the Library's web page

What is a database? - A database is a collection of information that has been organized so that it can be searched easily.

Conducting the Search (Example)

What is your PICO question?

Does the practice of acupuncture relieve pain in people who experience regular migraine headaches?

Record some keywords or terms that are important parts of your PICO question.

migraine headaches   *treatment*
acupuncture   *pain relief / migraines*

Example of Refine in writing (using the database CINAHL)

Initial Search Strategy	# of Results	Useful references?
treating migraine headaches (in default location to search)	7	No

Refined Search Strategy (e.g., Removed keyword)	# of Results	Useful references?
Add/Remove keywords migraine headaches (in default) AND treatment (in default)	251	Better
Edit search by adding "Limits" Check "peer reviewed" , "Evidence Based Practice" and Set years to 2007-2011	8	Yes

In the final 8 results, only one of the results was found in the original search that returned 7 results.

Is there an article in the final results that would work to answer your PICO question?

Tips / Things to Remember

Library Home Page -
www.uwec.edu/Library/

Ask us! If you have trouble or can't find what you need

Databases by Topic

Select best database for your research or select one of the multi-discipline databases

How many text boxes can you use to write your search?

How are those text boxes connected?

What is each text box searching in?

Adjust your keywords based on the way that the database refers to the topic

Read the abstract of an article for keywords that you may not have used

Is the article peer-reviewed?

"Limit your results"
You can select options to limit your results before you start the search.
Only get Peer Reviewed results
Only get Evidence-Based Practice results
Only get results that have a nurse as the first author or as any author
DO NOT SELECT "ONLY FULL TEXT"

Conduct your search

What is your PICO question?

Record some keywords or terms that are important parts of your PICO question.

Search/Refine Table

Use the boxes to indicate how you started and refined your search.

Initial Search Strategy	# of Results	Useful references?
Refined Search Strategy (e.g. Removed keyword)	**# of Results**	**Useful references?**

Selecting an Article

Things to consider when selecting an article.

Does it meet the requirements for your assignment?

How can you get access to the full text of the article?

Discuss with your group why you chose the article you did.

What problems did you have in finding an article?

Appendix L

Lesson Study in Nursing—Junior Worksheet

Example

PICO question: *In people receiving cardiopulmonary resuscitation (CPR), how does compression-only CPR compare with traditiional CPR in terms of survival rate?*

Keywords: *cardiopulmonary resuscitation, CPR, compression-only, traditional, survival rate*

Keywords searched: *CPR, survival rate*

Your
Group's:
    PICO
    question:

    Keywords:

Your group will now divide into two teams (A & B) and will search using the same topic and keywords but use different databases.

Both teams will need to record the first two articles they find, on the chart provided.

1) Compare CINAHL and Core Nursing Databases. (10 min.)

Team A will search the Core Nursing databases.

Team B will search in the CINAHL database.

Remember to use the same keywords for both searches.

Keywords searched:

First five words of article title:	Year published:	Level of evidence: I-VII or unsure:	Database	Nurse as author?	Peer-reviewed?
				Yes, No, or Unsure:	
			Core		
			Core		
			CINAHL		
			CINAHL		

2) Compare CINAHL with limits and Core Nursing Databases with Limits. (10 min.)

Team A will search the Core Nursing databases using limits.
Team B will search in the CINAHL database using limits.

Remember to use the same keywords for both searches.

Remember that your assignment's requirements are that the articles used should be:

Published within last 7 years.

A research article.

Written by a nurse.

Keywords searched:

First five words of article title:	Year published:	Level of evidence: I-VII or unsure:	Database	Yes, No, or Unsure:	
				Nurse as author?	Peer-reviewed?
			Core		
			Core		
			CINAHL		
			CINAHL		

3) Compare other Databases. (10 min.)

Team A will search Mosby's Nursing Consult **OR** PsycINFO.

Team B will search MEDLINE **OR** Nursing Reference Center.

Remember to use the same keywords for both searches.

Use all the search skills you have learned.

Keywords searched:

First five words of article title:	Year published:	Level of evidence: I-VII or unsure:	Database	Yes, No, or Unsure:	
				Nurse as author?	Peer-reviewed?

4) Class Discussion. (10 min)

1) Did both teams find the same first two articles? If not how do the articles differ? (i.e. Is one team's more relevant or applicable to the PICO question?)

2) Which database (Core Nursing or CINAHL) was easier to search when using limits?

3) Why did you choose your particular database in section three?

4) Were the results of the last search using your choice of database as good or better than the previous searches? Why?

5) If you could not find anything related to your PICO question with these searches, where would you look next or what would you do?

6) Does your PICO question need to be revised based on your search results? Why?

Appendix M

Lesson Study in Nursing—Senior Worksheet

Advanced Searching Exercise Nursing 472   Group Number: _____

Your group will work together to search different databases using the same topic and keywords.

Your Group's: PICO question:	
Keywords:	

1) Search PubMed (Database)

Entire team should work together to search database to find the best article for your PICO question.

Remember to use keywords from your PICO question.

EBP - Rating System for the Hierarchy of Evidence

I	Systematic Review (A synthesis of quasi experimental and/or correlational studies) or Meta-analysis (A review of randomized controlled trials)
II	Randomized Controlled Trial (Experimental study)
III	Controlled Trial Without Randomization (Quasi experimental)
IV	Case Controlled (Correlational) or Cohort Study (Descriptive)
V	Systematic reviews of descriptive and qualitative studies
VI	Descriptive or qualitative study
VII	Opinion of authorities and/or reports of expert committees

Keywords searched:	Revised keywords searched (If necessary):
# search results:	# search results:

First five words of article's title:	Year Published	Level of Evidence: I-VII?	Peer-reviewed? (Y/N/Unknown)
Best Article:			

2) Search National Guidelines Clearinghouse (Database)

Entire team should work together to identify best guideline for your PICO question.

Remember to use keywords from your PICO question.

Keywords searched:	Revised keywords searched (*If necessary*):
# search results:	# search results:

Full guideline's title:	Year Published	Reviewed & Reaffirmed (Date)	Level of Evidence: *
Best Guideline:			

* Note: Level of Evidence grading system may vary by guideline.

3) Search MedlinePlus (Database)

Entire team should work together to search database to find best resource.

Remember to use keywords from your PICO question.

EBP - Rating System for the Hierarchy of Evidence

I	Systematic Review (A synthesis of quasi experimental and/or correlational studies) or Meta-analysis (A review of randomized controlled trials)
II	Randomized Controlled Trial (Experimental study)
III	Controlled Trial Without Randomization (Quasi experimental)
IV	Case Controlled (Correlational) or Cohort Study (Descriptive)
V	Systematic reviews of descriptive and qualitative studies
VI	Descriptive or qualitative study
VII	Opinion of authorities and/or reports of expert committees

Keywords searched:

Revised keywords searched (*If necessary*):

search results:

search results:

First five words of resource's title:	Last Reviewed (Year)	Level of Evidence: I-VII?	Type of Resource †	Peer-reviewed? (Y/N/Unknown)
Best Resource:				

† Note: e.g. journal article, webpage, handout, multimedia, video, etc.

4) Class Discussion.

1) How did your PICO question work? Did you have to change it? Why? Did you use the same keywords for each search? If not why?

2) How will you use each database in your future nursing practice?
   a) PubMed

   b) National Guideline Clearinghouse

   c) MedlinePlus

3) What kind of data did you fill in when completing the "Type of Resource" column in the MedlinePlus worksheet section?

4) Which of the three databases used today would you search to answer the clinical question in each of the following scenarios?

COPD Scenario:

How might this patient manage his disease to prevent future exacerbations?

Where would you start looking for the answer? (circle one)

PubMed   National Guideline Clearinghouse   MedlinePlus

CHF Scenario:

How might you educate this patient about CHF to prevent further hospital admissions?

Where would you start looking for the answer? (circle one)

PubMed   National Guideline Clearinghouse   MedlinePlus

DM Scenario:

What education should she receive about better maintaining her glucose control to better manage her diabetes?

Where would you start looking for the answer? (circle one)

PubMed   National Guideline Clearinghouse   MedlinePlus

CVA Scenario:

What are interventions or treatments you will use with this patient if your Ischemic Stroke diagnosis is confirmed?

Where would you start looking for the answer? (circle one)

PubMed   National Guideline Clearinghouse   MedlinePlus

CAD Scenario:

What evidence is available that may inform how to best care for your patient with CAD?

Where would you start looking for the answer? (circle one)

PubMed   National Guideline Clearinghouse   MedlinePlus

Index

About the Authors

Jill Markgraf, professor and head of research and instruction at the University of Wisconsin–Eau Claire, has published and presented in the areas of library instruction, faculty collaboration, and distance education. She has worked and taught in academic libraries for more than twenty years.

Kate Hinnant, assistant professor, is a research and instruction librarian for the Business School at the University of Wisconsin–Eau Claire. In addition to working on the first "One-Shot" redesign, she also developed the supplementary research instruction and online lessons for the Blugold Seminar in Critical Reading & Writing.

Eric Jennings, associate professor, is an instruction and outreach librarian at the University of Wisconsin–Eau Claire. He has presented and published on integrating information literacy into the curriculum and on outreach activities within academic libraries.

Hans Kishel, associate professor, is a research and instruction librarian for the sciences at the University of Wisconsin–Eau Claire. He has presented and published in the areas of active learning and integrated information literacy instruction for many years. He is also a published game designer.